To
Alfred Meyer
With regards,
Roy Calby
1-16-68

CONQUEST WITH WORDS

How the Communist Lingo Promotes World Revolution

by
ROY COLBY

Foreword
by
HERBERT A. PHILBRICK

CRESTWOOD BOOKS
P. O. Box 2096
Arlington, Virginia 22202

. . . Communists still use Aesopian language; they say one thing and mean another. In this manner they fool non-communists, encouraging them to believe that communism stands for something desirable. The trained communist knows otherwise; it is more double talk with a completely different meaning. . . .

. . . Communism, in brief, has bitterly indicted communism; communist practice has indicted communist theory; communist actions have indicted the perverted use of such lofty words as "peace", "justice" and liberty." . . .

. . . They clothe themselves with everything good, noble and inspiring to exploit these ideals to their own advantage. . . .

J. EDGAR HOOVER
in *Masters of Deceit*

3

"Newspeak was the official language of Oceania and had been devised to meet the ideological needs of Ingsoc, or English Socialism. . . . The purpose of Newspeak was not only to provide a medium of expression for the world-view and mental habits proper to the devotees of Ingsoc, but to make all other modes of thought impossible. . . . Its vocabulary was so constructed as to give exact and often very subtle expression to every meaning that a Party member could properly wish to express, while excluding all other meanings and also the possibility of arriving at them by indirect methods."

—NINETEEN EIGHTY-FOUR
*by George Orwell
(Harcourt, Brace & Co.
New York, N.Y., 1949)*

TABLE OF CONTENTS

Foreword 7
Introduction 11
I   The Communist Lingo in Action 15
II   How Communists Express Double
      Meanings 23
III   Concepts and Judgments 31
IV   World Events Through Communist Eyes .. 37
V   Ideological Assumptions 44
VI   Words: Auxiliaries to Seizure and
      Communization 51
VII   Origins of the Communist Lingo 56
VIII A Rose by Any Other Name 63
IX   International Political Climates 72
X   "Peaceful Coexistence" in Three Months .. 78
XI   The Status Quo — Communist Style 86
XII   The Verbal Jungles of Vietnam 94
XIII The Communist Version of International
      Law 103
XIV   Semantics and the UN Charter 112
XV   The Language of "Revolution" in
      the U. S. 121
XVI   Understanding the Communist Lingo 131
Glossary of Communist Terminology
      Dictionary of Double Talk 139

5

About
Herbert A. Philbrick

Mr. Philbrick, citizen, "Communist", and counterspy, is a man who, according to TIME Magazine, "postponed his own life, liberty and pursuit of happiness, to get to the bottom of the great Communist conspiracy in the U. S." At the age of twenty-five this young Bostonian began, quite by accident, one of the most extraordinary adventures that has happened to any American in our time. It was to lead, nine years later, to the courtroom of Judge Harold R. Medina where Mr. Philbrick, the government's surprise witness, related the incredible story of his three lives as citizen, "Communist", and counterspy for the F.B.I.

He was chairman of a youth group in a Boston suburb only to discover that a group of young Communists had quietly "captured" the organization. Philbrick discussed his problem with the FBI, who suggested that he stay to discover the Communists' intentions.

His experiences inside the party were varied. He reorganized party cells in Boston suburbs, subverted the campaign of an anti-Communist candidate for Congress, taught revolutionary tactics in a secret school, organized the infiltration of an insurance company for a Communist-controlled union, and rewrote a speech for a presidential candidate. Finally, he was tapped for the party's inner circle, and joined the "Pro-4" group which master-minded strategy. There he met important Communist leaders and went underground for the most important work of his "Communist" career.

The perilous nine-year masquerade lasted until the FBI had enough evidence to spring the trap on the top eleven Communist leaders, who were brought to trial in New York in April 1949. He continued in the battle against the forces of totalitarian oppression wherever it exists, or wherever the liberty of free men is threatened.

Mr. Philbrick is presently National Director of the United States Anti-Communist Congress in Washington, D. C.

6

FOREWORD
BY
HERBERT A. PHILBRICK

IN THE FALL of 1967, Foreign News Correspondent F. Yorick Blumenfeld returned to the United States after a three-year tour of duty in the leading iron-curtain countries. He reported:

"Little of what I now hear in America about Eastern Europe, in fact, truly relates to the realities of Warsaw, Prague, or Budapest.

"Even some very sophisticated American observers prefer not to think in such revealing terms as the 'iron curtain' or 'police states'. Yet, merely wishing the curtain away . . . does not alter the fact of its existence. Numbers of East Germans, Czechs and Hungarians are still being shot trying to cross into Austria."

The people of the United States have access to more news media than any other nation in the world: thousands of daily and weekly newspapers, hundreds of magazines, thousands of radio and TV stations. Since this is true, why should their ideas about the Soviet-occupied nations not be in accord with reality?

I meet constantly with refugees who have recently fled from behind the iron curtain. Their most often repeated comment is: "You Americans just don't understand".

7

Why not?

Conquest With Words by Roy Colby provides an important clue — and perhaps the major clue — as to why the average American, with massive amounts of reading material at his disposal, is still confused about the most urgent and important issue of the day, that of Communism.

Literate humans maintain contact with reality largely through words and word symbols. True, knowledge is acquired through familiarity gained from actual experience, by touch, taste, vision, sound. But what we see, hear, taste or touch within the immediate vicinity of our bodies is very limited; we would know little, indeed, if it were not for modern mass communications media — radio, TV, newspapers, books, and magazines. By these devices we extend our scope of knowledge and information to encompass vast areas of the world which we will never see in person.

But whether spoken or read, the real world in which we live is made known to us by *words*.

Suppose, however, that the word symbols we read or hear are distorted, inaccurate, or untrue? Then, by the same token and to the same degree, our knowledge of the world is distorted, inaccurate and untrue.

Worse yet, what if some words which are accepted as having very clear and specific connotations and meanings, do in fact "mean" the *very opposite*? If and when this happens, our minds become in fact disconnected from the real world altogether, and "the mind's eye" carries an image of an unreal, untrue, non-existent world.

In dealing with the Communist world, we are forced to contend with both such distortions of reality. Experts have estimated that the Soviet Union spends something in excess of $3 billion a year on Communist propaganda designed for consumption (perhaps "absorption" is a better word) by the Free World. A great deal of this propaganda is deliberately designed to mislead and confuse the "capitalist enemy". In the Communist scheme to conquer the world, propaganda has become an aggressive and deadly weapon of greater and more devastating impact than bombs and bullets.

This year, in particular, will witness the most massive propaganda attack yet directed against the Free World. Marking the event of the greatest human-contrived disaster ever to befall mankind — the so called "1917 Bolshevik Revolution" — the Communists the world over will be producing and firing millions of words in our direction — words that can kill, in a very real sense. And the deadliest words of all will be those with double meanings: Communist lingo, comprised of word symbols that have one meaning to us but an entirely different meaning to the Communists. And a stepped up campaign to conquer more of the West with words can be expected next year . . . and during the decade ahead.

Thus, Mr. Colby's study of the Communist lingo could not be more timely nor more urgently deserving of our attention. Unless we understand exactly what the Communists are saying, every last one of us non-Communists and anti-Communists can be misled, can be duped, and in some cases can actually serve as "transmission belts" to convey the Communist lies and distortions to others. The only way we can comprehend the reality of Communism is to understand the language of Communism; and toward this understanding, Mr. Colby has made a major contribution. Such understanding will shift the odds in our favor to win.

About the Author

Roy Edward Colby brings a rich background of experience and education to bear in this volume on the problem of Communist gains through language perversion.

As a Foreign Service officer in the American Embassy in Havana, he saw Castro's Cuba unveil before his eyes. He witnessed the daily unfolding of the master plan to communize Cuba in which the entire communications system was used to achieve revolutionary ends.

Mr. Colby served as an intelligence officer in World War II in Morocco, Algeria and Italy. Following nine years as an official in the International Educational Exchange Service, Department of State (1946-55), Mr. Colby spent the next seven years in the U. S. Foreign Service in Brazil, Mexico and Cuba. He was forced to leave when Castro came to power in 1961. Mr. Colby has been teaching Spanish at Colorado State College, Greeley, since 1962.

He has done research in the comparison of various aspects of Western and revolutionary semantics, ethics and logic. His articles have appeared in U. S. NEWS & WORLD REPORT, RALLY MAGAZINE, ELKS MAGAZINE, THE NEW GUARD and HUMAN EVENTS.

Mr. Colby holds B.A. and M.A. degrees from Ohio University, *Magna cum Laude,* Phi Beta Kappa, and an M.A. Degree in Romance Languages, University of Michigan. He is active in civic affairs.

Thus, Mr. Colby writes from the vantage point of an eyewitness, a research worker in semantics, an educator in language and a student of contemporary problems of Communism.

10

INTRODUCTION

I spent the latter part of 1960 in Castro's Cuba.

As a Foreign Service officer assigned to the American Embassy in Havana, one of my duties was to prepare and forward to Washington reports on those Cuban activities which affected American business and trade. At that time there was a great deal to report because the Cuban Revolutionary Government, as it was called, was engaged in a massive, systematic effort to drive all American business interests out of Cuba and take over their properties. This successful effort, as we know so well in unerring retrospect, was part of a well laid and well executed plan to gain complete control of the country's economy and make Cuba the first Communist state in Latin America.

During my tour-of-duty, which ended abruptly with the breaking of diplomatic relations in January 1961, I observed several things which were puzzling but at the same time fascinating. For example, government censorship permitted only one version to be given to the events taking place inside Cuba. Early in the communization process, the Castro regime had seized control of the communications media. Newspapers, magazines, radio and television broadcasts, as well as telephone, telegraph and postal services, were under the firm control of the Communists. Insofar as possible, only information favorable to the Revolutionary Government was permitted to circulate on the island.

11

Moreover, the United States, which had aided Castro to overthrow the Cuban dictator, Fulgencio Batista, was being subjected to a full-fledged "hate campaign", similar to the one now being conducted against us by Red China. We were the "Yankee imperialists" who exploited the downtrodden Cuban people. We were poised to invade Cuba at any moment. We were the "Yankee exploiters" whose business and industrial monopolies were sucking the life-blood of the people.

With no regard for the facts which proved the contrary, everything we did, it seemed, was bad, wrong and reactionary, while everything the "glorious Cuban Revolutionary Government" did was good, right and progressive.

In four words, "Cuba sí, Yankee no!"

Futhermore, all seizures of American property were made legally — from the Communist viewpoint — under authority of some specific order or decree issued by the Cuban Revolutionary Government. Although plausible reasons were often given for the expropriation of U.S. firms, some of the reasons were not true.

Take the incident of the American tire factory. One morning in the fall of 1960, a group of bearded Cuban soldiers, armed with Czech submachineguns, marched into the manager's office and announced, "We are nationalizing this tire factory in the name of the Cuban Revolutionary Government. You have one hour to clear out."

Although the factory manager was looking into the business end of several submachineguns, he was courageous enough to ask under what authority the takeover was being made. The leader of the Cuban soldiers handed him a copy of a nationalization decree, in which it was stated that tire production had fallen off in recent months, which was considered detrimental to the national interest. For this reason, the factory had been ordered to be nationalized .

"But," the manager protested, "this isn't true. Our records show that tire production has increased, not decreased."

"Capitalist lies," snapped the leader of the machine-gun squad. "The decree tells the truth. It says that tire production has decreased and therefore it has decreased. Get out!"

So the manager got out and his factory was nationalized.

This incident gave me food for thought. The image of a bearded Cuban with a machinegun haunted me. "Capitalist lies," he had said, even in the face of concrete evidence to the contrary. "The decree tells the truth. . ." The "truth". The "truth" of the decree and the "truth" of the tire factory's statistics were contradictory. What was the "truth"?

And what made these people so consistent in their attacks against the United States? Could it be possible that they really believed what they were saying? Was there some sort of logic behind this barrage of obviously false charges and accusations, which the U.S. government took very seriously and attempted to refute? Did they employ some sort of Orwellian "newspeak", intelligible to the initiated but confusing and irrational to the Western mind? Although not realizing it at the time, I had been exposed to a new way of making judgments, expressed in an unfamiliar communications system and based on a moral and ethical code completely different from ours.

A subsequent study of Communist semantics revealed that this communications system — this Communist lingo — was the language of world revolution and inextricably bound up with the theories, objectives and practices of the international Communist movement. It also became evident that the Communist lingo was capable of transmitting simultaneously two different messages, one for the non-Communist world and the other for the Communist world. We in the West fail to understand what Communists are really driving at because we tend to interpret their words at face value, not realizing the ulterior meanings implicit in them.

My study also led me to assemble an American-style Russian dictionary which explains the ulterior meaning of Communist terms.

I am particularly indebted to Dr. Stefan T. Possony, Director of International Studies, Hoover Institution, Stanford, California for two excellent pamphlets on Communist semantics, which I found invaluable in preparing this book. They are: *Wordsmanship — Semantics as a Communist Weapon,* prepared for the Senate Internal Security Subcommittee in 1961, and *Language as a Communist Weapon,* prepared in consultation with Dr. Possony by the Committee on Un-American Activities in 1959. Both pamphlets were published by the U.S. Government Printing Office, Washington, D. C.

Roy Colby
Greeley, Colorado

November 1967

CHAPTER I

THE COMMUNIST LINGO IN ACTION

> "What's the use of repeating all that stuff," the
> Mock Turtle interrupted, "if you don't explain it
> as you go on? It's by far the most confusing
> thing *I* ever heard."
>
> —*Alice in Wonderland*

The radio announcer had just described the excesses
taking place in Red China. "According to an ideological organ of the Chinese Communist Party," he went
on, "the Red Guards are considered to be 'the hope of
the proletariat' — whatever that means!" he ad-libbed
with evident relish.

Far from being a joke, the bit of information contained in the phrase, "the hope of the proletariat", may
have been a veiled prophecy of considerable significance to the West. The thought was couched in the
Communist lingo, however, which apparently caused
the amusement of the newscaster. In the Fall of 1966
when the incident occurred, the Red Guards were on
a rampage of terror and violence trying to propagate
"the thoughts of Mao" and also eliminate opposition to
the "cultural revolution", that is to say, Mao's policies.

Due to the effectiveness of the pyramidal power
structure in the Communist hierarchy known as "democratic centralism", few policy statements are issued in
any official Communist publication without the bless-

15

ings of the top Communist. Here then, in effect, was
what Mao was saying, "I have pinned my hopes on the
Red Guards' ability to eliminate opposition to my
policies. If they fail. . ."

"Proletariat" is a revolutionary term which means
"people", which means "Communists", which means
"the Communist Party", which in Red China means
Mao Tse-Tung. In other words, "the hope of the proletariat" is in reality the hope of the one man who
controls the proletariat, the people, the other Communists and the Party.

The Red Guards were not successful in carrying out
Mao's mission. By midsummer 1967 evidence had
filtered through the Bamboo Curtain indicating that
Red China was in the throes of a huge civil war.

"Peace for Our Grandchildren"

The leaders of the two most powerful nations on
earth recently came to an agreement, a minor one to
be sure, but nevertheless an agreement.

Following the first Glassboro summit meeting in
June 1967, President Johnson was quoted as saying
that although he reached no new agreements with
Soviet Premier Kosygin, "he and I agreed that we
wanted a world of peace for our grandchildren." This
was news of the first water and the press throughout the
nation gave it such prominence that newspaper readers
could easily have concluded that this was the most
important result of the meeting. One newspaper, for
example, came out with a five-column, front-page
headline, LBJ, KOSYGIN BOTH SEEK 'PEACE
FOR GRANDCHILDREN'.

Here is a classic example of how effective the Communist lingo can be in influencing American public

opinion. Of course the "world of peace" the President wants will be free from war and hostilities. Of course the all-Communist "world of peace" the premier was thinking of will be free from war and hostilities.

Since in its revolutionary sense an "agreement" always brings strength to the Communist side, how did the Soviet Union benefit? Perhaps the answer is contained in the answer to another question: How many thousands, or millions — who knows? — of Americans came to believe that nice, grandfatherly Mr. Kosygin's "peacefully coexisting" Soviet Union wants the same kind of peace they do?

Peace — who doesn't want it? But which kind?

When Can LBJ Return Kosygin's Visit?

A few hours after the second Glassboro summit meeting, Premier Kosygin returned to New York City where he held a press conference during which he was asked the following question: "Will President Johnson receive the same warm welcome given to you in this country if he should visit the Soviet Union?" This was his reply: "Why, I believe that if aggression were ended and a truly peaceful policy pursued, the welcome that the President would receive in the Soviet Union would be very cordial indeed."

If one stops a moment to think about it, isn't this an amazing statement to make about a nation that shuns aggression like the plague and bends over backwards to bring peace to the world? If one reflects another moment, however, he will realize the Communist leader used "aggression" and "peaceful policy" in their revolutionary sense.

When Kosygin's comments are translated from the Communist lingo it becomes apparent that President

Johnson would receive a cordial welcome in Soviet Russia if, for example, the United States should withdraw its troops unconditionally from Southeast Asia, join in condemning Israel as the aggressor in the Middle East, and take other steps to demonstrate its support of Soviet foreign policy.

A Morally Unstable . . . a Sick Person

On her arrival in the United States, Svetlana Alliluyeva, defected daughter of the late Soviet dictator, Josef Stalin, explained her defection in these words, "Since my childhood I have been taught communism. . . but. . . I found it was impossible to exist without God."

This explanation for her change of attitude makes sense to most Americans, who would probably agree that Svetlana is a normal human being with high moral standards. It is therefore significant to take note of the Communist evaluation of Stalin's daughter made by one of the highest ranking Russian Marxist-Leninists. At his previously mentioned press conference, Premier Kosygin made this observation, ". . . I want to say the following: Alliluyeva is a morally unstable person and she is a sick person."

Any person, then, especially an influential defector to the West who rejects the atheistic Communist ethic in favor of morality based on belief in God, may be properly represented as being in need of psychiatric care.

All My Boys Could Not Breathe

In 1964 following a decisive loss to the U.S. men's track team in a meet held in Los Angeles, the Soviet track coach complained to reporters that the defeat "was not because the Russians could not run faster"; it was, of all things, "the Los Angeles smog."

"All my boys could not breathe," he said.

This charge naturally sent the Los Angeles Air Polution Control into a tizzy of indignation and denials. An investigation disclosed there had been nothing wrong with the Los Angeles air during the track meet. Supposing there had been? Wouldn't it have affected the Russian women, whose team defeated their American opponents in the same meet? Many newspaper readers undoubtedly passed off the complaint as poor sportsmanship.

The Marxist-Leninist track coach, however, knew exactly what he was doing. He was not interested in such "bourgeois" concepts as "good sportsmanship". As might be expected, he vocalized his thoughts in the Communist lingo in which the "truth" is anything that advances the Cause. How did this seemingly absurd complaint do it? Here's how:

(1) It denied that the Soviet male athlete is inferior to the American male athlete.

(2) It presented the enemy in a bad light. Since naturally there is no admittable smog in any "socialist" state, therefore "Socialism" is better than Capitalism.

(3) The story was carried abroad by the international wire services, both Communist and non-Communist. Which version of the event was believed? In other countries the question must have lingered, unanswered: Were the Soviet trackmen *really* affected by the Los Angeles smog?

Who's Schizophrenic?

Several years ago after one of the meetings of the

perennial Disarmament Conference, a Western negotiator charged that the Russians had gone to Geneva
without being prepared for any serious talks and that
the Soviet position against international inspection was
"schizophrenic". He also pointed out that the Soviet
negotiator devoted most of his time to a denunciation
of American policy in Vietnam and other unrelated
issues.

The Soviet Union, on the contrary, did precisely
what it agreed to do. This large Communist state had
"agreed" to "negotiate" disarmament, i.e., to extract
some advantages for the Cause in the general field of
disarmament. Far from being schizophrenic, the Soviet
position on international inspection was quite practical
for at least three reasons:

(1) Hopefully, the revolutionary view of disarmament might eventually be accepted, i.e., that the West
should disarm unilaterally, trusting the Soviet Union
to follow suit.

(2) In the meantime, the Conference offered an
admirable international forum for dispensing anti-
American propaganda.

(3) The eventual failure of the Conference, in
case the West did not give in, could somehow be
blamed on the U.S.

Persecution or British Justice?

The following item appeared in the *New York Times*
for July 22, 1967: "The Peking radio announced
tonight that Anthony Grey, the Reuters correspondent,
would be forbidden to leave his residence until further
notice as a reprisal for the 'unjustified persecution' of
Chinese Communist reporters in Hong Kong." Readers
were left wondering about the nature of the "unjustified

persecution" which had evoked the reprisal. The rest of the news item gave no explanation.

The key to interpreting the incident may be found in the revolutionary meanings of "unjustified persecution" and "reprisal". In keeping with the Communist lexicon, the use of force by non-Communist military or civil authorities to prevent illegal Communist acts is considered (a) "unjustified" (because it hinders the Cause) and (b) "persecution" (because force is used) and (c) therefore subject to "reprisal".

One with some knowledge of the Communist lingo could logically infer that the Reuters correspondent was put under house arrest in Peking because the British police in Hong Kong had arrested some Chinese Communist newspapermen who had broken the law, perhaps by instigating or participating in the Communist-led riots which were going on at the time.

And this was exactly what happened. Later dispatches from Hong Kong stated that the British government had banned three Communist Hong Kong newspapers and arrested a number of staff members for sedition.

Building Socialism in Algeria

Colonel Houari Boumedienne overthrew "President" Ben Bella in June 1965, thus offering hope to the West that perhaps Algeria's leftward plunge would be halted. In his first nationwide address following his ascent to power, Boumedienne pledged Algeria's "cooperation with all peoples in mutual respect for national sovereignty". Thus in the Communist lingo Ben Bella's successor informed Communists everywhere (all peoples) that Algeria planned to steer an independent course between the Soviet Union and Red China.

Boumedienne later described Ben Bella's concentration of power into his own hands as a form of "deviationism", employing the same term that Red Chinese leader Mao Tse-Tung later used against those who disagreed with him. Ben Bella did not follow the proper course, i.e., the Party Line, in "building Socialism" in (communizing) Algeria, Boumedienne said. As further justification for the ouster, Boumedienne used other Communist terms. He accused Ben Bella of having established "the cult of the hero", and "the cult of the popular idol", variations of "the cult of the personality" which Khrushchev had leveled against the dead Stalin and which, in turn, Brezhnev and Kosygin leveled against the deposed Khrushchev.

Those who understood the Communist lingo, of course, knew immediately that the new leader of Algeria planned to continue the communization of the country begun by Ben Bella.

Addressing himself to the problem of understanding the Communist lingo, Dr. Stefan T. Possony, a recognized authority on Communist semantics and Director of International Studies at Stanford University's Hoover Institution, made the following comment to a Senate Subcommittee in 1961:

"Naturally the average American cannot perform analyses of this type [such as given in this chapter] without becoming a full-time expert. He cannot change his profession but he should insist that our decision-makers become fully aware of semantic trickery and clarify for the American people the real meaning of Communist doubletalk."[1]

---

[1] *Wordsmanship — Semantics as a Communist Weapon,* prepared for the Senate Internal Security Subcommittee, U. S. Government Printing Office, Washington, D. C., 1961.

CHAPTER II

HOW COMMUNISTS
EXPRESS DOUBLE MEANINGS

"Every Communist message must convey an orthodox, that is, revolutionary activating message to the party and its followers. This same communication must convey a different, i.e., soothing, pacifying and paralyzing message to the opponent of communism."

—Stefan T. Possony

Fortunately, Western leaders and political observers seem to be becoming increasingly aware that the words used by Communists have restricted meanings often far removed from normal usage. They are commencing to realize that such terms as aggression, imperialism, wars of national liberation, independence movements, neo-colonialism, neutrality, democracy, peace, peaceful coexistence and peaceful settlement lose their absolute quality and take on an ideological tinge when voiced by Communist spokesmen.

Indeed, some words are twisted to such an extent that their meaning comes out completely opposite to their generally accepted sense. For example, Communists would have the world believe the United States is committing "imperialist aggression" in Vietnam and not trying to preserve the freedom and independence of a sovereign state which had requested our help. In

23

a similar vein, last summer the Soviet Union tried to have the United Nations condemn as "aggression" the successful efforts of Israel to defend itself against threated destruction.

Futhermore, when Communists take action it is always good — from their point of view. If the United States should do the same thing, however, it would be "bad". The flagrant interference of the Soviet Union, Red China, Cuba and other Communist states into the internal affairs of non-Communist countries is accordingly justified by such noble phrases as "wars of national liberation" or "independence movements" expressing "the will of the people" seeking "self-determination". If the shoe were on the other foot, the Communist propagandists would shrilly accuse the United States of intervention, imperialism, neo-colonialism, warmongering, aggression and a host of other things suggestive of violations of international law and breaches of the peace. As a matter of fact, Communists use these very phrases to describe our efforts to curb their aggression!

Suzanne Labin summarized her thoughts on this kind of word-twisting, which she calls "a veritable semantic war", as follows:

"That we, in the West, label as 'neutralist' regimes such as the one which reigned in Indonesia under Sukarno and in Ceylon, Ghana, Egypt, Algeria, Cambodia, etc., countries which systematically and ostentatiously support the Communist bloc against the Western bloc, is in truth a scandal. It gives additional testimony to the intellectual abdication of the West, which, without resistance, has allowed the Communists to pervert every word and concept carrying some prestige: democracy, peace, progressiveness and, of most recent vintage, neutralism."[1]

Here then, succinctly put, is the heart of the difficulty. Words do not mean the same for Communists; they have a special revolutionary significance. Hence, the West confuses the dictionary meaning with the ideological meaning inherent in Communist utterances. But Communists are not confused; they understand *both* meanings and capitalize on the confusion and temporary support of deceived non-Communists.

Following are some examples showing how the Communist lingo works and how it is used to promote the policies of the Soviet Union and other Communist states bent on world revolution.

Agreement With Western Action Brings "Praise"

In a joint statement issued by representatives of the United States, Great Britain and the Soviet Union, the limited nuclear test ban treaty signed in Moscow on August 8, 1963 was declared to be an "important initial step toward the lessening of international tensions and the strengthening of peace".

It is difficult to find fault with this statement, which at first glance appears to express sentiments that all nations, Communists and non-Communist alike, are in favor of. Everybody wants to see international tensions reduced and who doesn't want peace?

Yet this is not what the declaration implies to the Communist world.

Secretary of State Rusk and British Foreign Secretary Douglas-Home, the two non-Communist representatives to test ban parley, meant exactly what they said and

1 *Red Foxes in the Chicken Coop,* Suzanne Labin, Crestwood Books, Arlington, Va., 1966.

nothing more when *they* agreed to the joint declaration. When *he* agreed to the statement, however, Soviet Foreign Minister Gromyko employed the Communist lingo, which enabled him to speak out of both sides of his mouth at once, as it were. While paying lip service to the obvious meaning of the statement, he also was able to convey another message to Communists everywhere in the world. This message read as follows: "The United States is doing what we want them to do, and they will do other things we want them to do, thus bringing us closer to our goal of world domination."

How can such a different meaning be extracted from the hopeful declaration that the treaty represents an "important initial step toward the lessening of international tensions and the strengthening of peace"?

As Communists see it, "international tensions" can be lessened only when the enemy (in this case, the United States) yields to Soviet wishes. The Soviet Union wanted a test ban treaty and the United States obligingly cooperated. This was deemed to be an "important initial step", suggesting that future American actions would also be pleasing to the Soviet Union. In this context, the ulterior meaning of "peace" implies adoption of Western policy favorable to promotion of the Communist cause of world revolution, frequently shortened to "the Cause". Hence, from the Soviet viewpoint our signing the treaty actually helped the Communists along their march toward world domination.

The Essence of the Communist Lingo

As pointed out, Gromyko was able to transmit the

two diverse messages simultaneously by employing the Communist lingo, a precise, logical system of communications. It is called a lingo because it is a style of speech strange to the Western mind. It is a strange style of speech because all events, incidents and happenings assume revolutionary significance by being represented so as to put Communists in a favorable light and the non-Communists in an unfavorable one — except when the latter help advance the Cause. In such cases, Communists appear to praise the West, as was illustrated by the test ban treaty declaration.

This propaganda lingo has often been called "double-talk" because terms have ideological meanings paralleling the dictionary meanings. It is based on the Marxist-Leninist interpretation of the concept "truth". The test for Marxist-Leninist truth is a simple one: any utterance which advances revolutionary objectives is considered to be true, no matter how contradictory, absurd or contrary to the facts it may appear to non-Communists. This may account for the depreciatory labels — jabberwocky, argot, jargon, gobbledegook, "just Communist propaganda" and so on — applied to the Communist lingo by those who do not understand it. It seems to be a human trait to make fun of that which we understand imperfectly.

One of the basic principles underlying the application of the Communist lingo is: agreement and praise when any event promotes the cause of world revolution, and disagreement and condemnation when the Cause is being set back.

When an event has taken place, two determinations have to be made by Communist propaganda spokesmen: (1) In what way can the event be represented to promote the Cause? and (2) What degree of praise or condemnation shall be employed?

Disagreement With Western Action Brings Condemnation

We have already illustrated Communist agreement and implicit "praise" of the United States and Great Britain for signing a treaty with the Soviet Union.

The following example illustrates disagreement and condemnation of American action in the Caribbean:

In the Spring of 1965, U.S. Marines landed in Santo Domingo.

Tass, the Soviet news agency, termed the landings a "new and aggressive act of U.S. imperialism". The Red Chinese immediately charged that "thousands of U.S. Marines have landed and are slaughtering Dominican citizens". The Communist newspaper, *Hoy,* of Havana, said that "The United States intervention has, as always, been cynical, shameless and monstrous." The United States Communist Party issued a statement calling the landings "a blatant act of imperialist intervention", intended "to prevent the establishment of a democratic and popular government". Comment from other Communist sources was in a similar vein: all without exception condemned the American action in varying degrees of intensity.

Let us try to visualize the event from the Communist viewpoint. Dominican Communists, trained in Cuba and armed with Soviet bloc weapons, had planned to take advantage of an uprising and seize control of the Dominican government. The landing of the Marines, then, thwarted an attempted Communist takeover.

It logically follows that all comments by the Communist press, from whatever country, had to be critical. The U.S. action was detrimental to the Cause. Hence, we were in the wrong and should be condemned. The major decision for propagandists to make dealt only with the degree of intensity of the condemnation.

The Soviet Union, which was "coexisting peacefully" with the United States at the time, naturally had to exercise more restraint than the militant Red Chinese, who believe that "peaceful coexistence" is the wrong road to world revolution. To Soviet propagandists, the landings were a "new and aggressive act of U. S. imperialism". In its revolutionary sense, "aggressive" means the enemy used force to oppose a Communist advance. The term "imperialism" is normally evoked in connection with the U.S. military presence, for whatever reason, in any foreign country. This "aggressive" act was "new" because we had previously opposed Communist expansion in other areas of the world, e.g., in Korea in the early 1950's, during the 1962 Cuban missile crisis, in the Congo in 1964 when we airlifted American missionaries out of the country and, of course, our present "aggression" in Vietnam.

Red China pulled out all stops in charging that the Marines were "slaughtering Dominican citizens". It is a mistake to believe that all Communist utterances are meant for our ears alone. This crude and preposterous accusation may appear more credible to the captive citizens in Communist and "Socialist" states who get only one side of the news, and to those people of Asia, Africa and Latin America who have been conditioned by Communist propaganda to believe the worst about the United States.

The wrath and virulence of the Havana press are understandable since the U.S. action nullified a major

Cuban effort to export revolution to the Dominican Republic. Under these circumstances, all the accusations and charges — true or false — the Cuban Communists could level against the United States, in their frustration and disappointment, were obviously considered justified. It is quite in keeping with revolutionary logic to call the United States "cynical, shameless and monstrous" in this context.

Spokesmen for the Communist Party, U.S.A., apparently felt the best way of expressing their ideological version of what happened was to denounce the landings as a "blatant act of imperialist intervention". In this connection, it should be noted that armed opposition to a Communist takeover is deemed to be "intervention", which in this case was called "imperialist" because the United States was involved. It is literally true that President Johnson's intention was "to prevent the establishment of a democratic and popular government" because the revolutionary meaning of both "democratic" and "popular" is "Communist". The President, however, expressed the idea in Western thought: to prevent the Communists from seizing the government of the Dominican Republic.

If the revolutionary meanings are analyzed, it becomes evident that all the denunciations were true in the sense assigned to them in the Communist dictionary.

CHAPTER III

CONCEPTS AND JUDGMENTS

> "The truth in Russia is what the government says it is."
> —Jeane Claude Vierne, French chemical engineer who spent 1963 in the Soviet Union.

"He's got 'funny ideas'."

We sometimes apply this slangy expression to a person whose ways of looking at things are different from our own. Such a person could just as well have been described as saying, "He's got funny concepts" or "He uses unusual concepts in his thinking."

For, according to the dictionary, a concept is "an idea of what a thing in general should be".

Concepts are important. They are important because they play a crucial role in the formation of judgments, those decisions we make every day of our lives to guide our actions. The stringing together of concepts in a logical fashion is a major function of language.

Western Ideas of Goodness-Rightness

The following hypothetical event will serve to illustrate the importance of concepts in enabling us to interpret things rationally and uniformly:

"While robbing a bank, a man kills a bank employee in cold blood. Several outraged citizens pursue, capture and turn the robber over to the police."

31

First of all, we may make an overall judgment of the event. We may reason that, although the man committed robbery and murder (bad and wrong), he was apprehended (good and right) and undoubtedly will pay for his crimes (good and right). Despite the fact that we deplore crime, we would probably adjudge the net result as good and right because justice will undoubtedly be done and future bank robbers may be discouraged from breaking the law.

It will be noted that several corollary judgments are made as we draw the conclusion that, under the circumstances, the overall effect of the event was good and right. We adjudge murder and robbery as bad and wrong and the lawbreaker's apprehension as good and right. We arrive at both the principle and corollary judgments on the basis of our unconscious assumptions of what goodness, badness, rightness and wrongness should be.

Communist Ideas of Goodness-Rightness

We would certainly say that anyone who disagrees with these judgments has "funny ideas". In fact, it would hardly occur to us that the event or any of its elements could be interpreted in any other way. But different judgments are possible if other people have different ideas about the nature of goodness, badness, rightness and wrongness.

For purposes of illustration, let us assume that the "bankrobbing incident" took place, not in the United States in the year 1967, but in Tsarist Russia in the year 1909. Let us further assume that it was a Bolshevik conspirator who took the money from the bank, caused the death of the bank teller, was pursued, apprehended and turned over to the police. However, he was not any ordinary lawbreaker; he was acting on behalf of the cause of the Workers' Revolution (now called the Cause) aimed at overthrowing the Russian government. In the eyes of his fellow conspirators, did he rob? He did not. He used "extra-legal means" to acquire funds for the Cause. Did he kill? He did not. He merely liquidated an enemy of the Cause who was preventing him from accomplishing his objective. Was it good and right for him to try to advance the Cause in this manner? It was. Was it bad and wrong for him to be apprehended? It was. Would justice have been done if he were tried, convicted and punished for robbery and murder? No, indeed. Justice, in that case, would have been perverted.

Overall judgment? Bad and wrong for the Cause.

Even a half century ago, Communists had "funny ideas".

They still do.

Take the case of the foreign planes that landed in an African country in 1964. The Soviet bloc planes carrying war material for the Congolese revolutionaries were represented as the "forces of liberation". In the same year, American planes rescued several hundred white missionaries from the hands of the Communist-incited Congolese terrorists. These planes, however, represented the "forces of aggression". Yes, the Communists have "funny ideas" about such things as "liberation" and "aggression", which are expressed in the Communist lingo.

It was noted that their lingo is a strange style of speech because events are represented so as to put the Communists in a favorable light and the non-Communists in an unfavorable one. The "funny ideas" that Communists have — their concepts — stem from an ideological interpretation of what "truth" is. As we have seen, the Communists brand of truth is that which promotes the Cause and hence, conforms to a unique and restricted kind of reality. The judgments expressed in the lingo with which Communists verbalize their interpretation of events are necessarily related to their politically-oriented concepts.

Bases for Communist Judgments

Listed below are two classes of Communist concepts having opposite meanings. The "Positive Concepts", expressing goodness-rightness, form the basis of judgments made with respect to events or the acts of people (including individuals, groups, organizations and nations) that tend to benefit the Cause. The "Negative Concepts", denoting badness-wrongness, are the storehouse of ideas from which expressions of disapproval, condemnation and censure are withdrawn when the Cause is being impeded.

Positive Concepts	*Negative Concepts*
goodness	badness
rightness	wrongness
truth	falsity
progress	reaction
morality	anti-morality
justice	injustice
fairness	unfairness
reasonableness	unreasonableness
honesty	dishonesty
friendliness	unfriendliness
wisdom	folly

Example: Capitalism is bad.

Since saying this is in the interests of the Cause, the statement contains "truth" and Communists automatically draw on the "Positive Concepts" for other judgments. Besides being "true", the statement, therefore, is also good, right, progressive, moral, just, fair, reasonable, honest, friendly and wise.

Example: Communism is bad.

By the same process of logic, this statement is adjudged to be "false" and also bad, wrong, reactionary, anti-moral, unjust, unfair, unreasonable, dishonest, unfriendly and foolish.

Communist Truth Is Not Always Obvious

However, judgments are not ordinarily expressed so simply in the Communist lingo. One would more likely hear something like this:

"All intellectually honest men agree that imperialism breeds aggression." Or, "Only bourgeois ideologists and the politically uneducated fail to recognize the inherent advantage of Socialism."

It is interesting to translate the revolutionary meanings of the two statements. "Intellectually honest men" refers to those favorable to Communism. By definition, "imperialism" can be practiced only by powerful non-Communist states and, specifically, by the United States. We have already observed that "aggression" is non-Communist force which blocks Communist expansion. Thus, the first statement reads, in translation, as follows:

"All people friendly to Communism agree that the United States prevents Communist aggression by using force."

The thought contained in the second statement

emerges from the Marxist-Leninist labyrinth somewhat as follows:

"Only experts on Communism (bourgeois ideologists) and those who have not been duped, indoctrinated or brainwashed (the politically uneducated) fail to recognize the inherent advantages of Communism (Socialism)."

Thus what Communists represent in their lingo as being true is two-faced: (1) what they would like us to believe and (2) a frank admission of the facts of the matter for the information and instruction of other Communists.

CHAPTER IV

WORLD EVENTS THROUGH COMMUNIST EYES

> "Unquestionably, the American people do not bear malice toward the Soviet people; but they *know* that the words of Soviet leaders, the words of Communists, are not the words used in the language of true democracy and freedom."
> *Peaceful Coexistence — A Communist Blueprint for Victory.* (Reproduced by permission of the American Bar Association 1964.)

An event is a happening, occurrence or incident, usually a noteworthy one. In its broadest sense, an event is anything that takes place anywhere at any time. Literally billions of events take place all over the world every day. Everything that everyone of the world's three and a half billion inhabitants does could be construed as an event. Practically all of them are, of course, insignificant or trivial to the Western way of thinking. Only the smallest fraction of them are noteworthy — only when man bites dog, so to speak. But not insofar as Communists are concerned. Nothing that happens is so insignificant or trivial that it cannot be represented appropriately in the Communist lingo so as to advance the Cause in some measure. *All* events have potential political value, if exploited properly.

Events, then, are of great importance to world revolution.

People are important, too, because they are either participants in events or are affected by them.

As previously noted, Communists have their own special brand of concepts — their "funny ideas" about what things should be. Communist propagandists try to relate as many events and people as possible to their version of the basic concepts of goodness-rightness and badness-wrongness. In other words, attempts are made to reduce everything that promotes the Cause to the concept of goodness-rightness and, conversely, everything that hinders it, to the concept of badness-wrongness.

And even when the Cause is obviously being set back, the Communists, like Pollyanna, can find some "goodness" in it. The "good" may take a negative form. For example, the "good" that came out of the Communist setback in their attempt to overthrow the Dominican Republic government in the Spring of 1965 was the denunciation of the "badness-wrongness" ("intervention" and "imperialism") of the United States action of sending in the Marines.

On the other hand, even when the West cooperates (e.g., by signing the nuclear test ban treaty in 1963) by promoting the Cause (by definition, a treaty is a means of gaining strength), the praise given may be tempered by referring to a "triumph of men of sober judgment" over the "wild men" and "warmongering elements" in the "imperialist camp".

To the Communists, where events take place and who participates in them are decisive. To illustrate how the skillful use of the Communist lingo may serve to extract maximum benefit for the Cause from diverse happenings, two versions are given below for several random occurrences. In Version A, the United States is represented as being responsible for the event, or is being talked about. In Version B, the Communists are portrayed as being responsible for the event, or they are being talked about. Keep in mind where the events take place and who is involved. Note also how concepts are suggested in each event.

Interpretations of Events Promote the Cause

1. *A leaf falls.*

Version A. The photograph shows a lone scraggy tree in the slum district of a large American city. The depressing background of dirty tenement houses reflects drabness, despair and misery. A single leaf has fallen to the sidewalk. Even the leaves die in the capitalist police-state where the vultures of Wall Street suck the lifeblood of the downtrodden masses.

Version B. Another photograph shows another tree in another city in another country. But what do we see here? A shining new Workers' Apartment Building in the background. A single leaf has fallen to the sidewalk. This fallen leaf will, of course, be immediately swept up by that eager streetcleaner, diligently doing his part to keep this beautiful Socialist city clean.

2. *A baby cries.*

Version A. Why is this ragged, half-starved Vietnamese baby crying? Because his mother has been wantonly murdered by a bomb dropped by the heartless American imperialists, who are escalating their acts of terror and aggression against the peaceloving people of Vietnam. Go home, Yankee, go home, and let the sovereign Vietnamese people resolve their political differences in a peaceful manner.

Version B. Why is this well-fed baby crying? He is merely hungry, as all healthy babies are near feeding time. Soon the nurse of the Boys' Section of the State Home for Children of Socialist Workers will give him nourishing food. In the meantime, he is learning to develop patience, an attribute common to the progressive Socialist people. One day soon, his mother will leave the collective farm where she has been willingly doing her share to keep the state granaries filled and pay her child a visit. Hush, my baby, hush!

3. *A boy reads*.

Version A. The slovenly boy is American. The book is a cheap paperback. On the cover is a half-naked woman lying in a pool of blood. This is the way delinquents and school-dropouts employ their idle time in the decadent capitalistic states. No wonder they have such a high crime rate!

Version B. This studious Soviet teenager, however, is reading a history book. He is doing his homework. He is learning how Lenin, their glorious leader, established the progressive Union of Soviet Socialist Republics.

4. *Students riot*.

Version A. These progressive California students are being denied their constitutional right of free speech and are subjected to unreasonable and dictatorial discipline by a reactionary and undemocratic college administration.

Version B. These reactionary African students falsely charge racial discrimination in the Soviet Union. As everybody knows, this is absurd. These unruly hooligans, these troublemaking elements, can leave the country at any time if they do not like Soviet laws and insist on disturbing the public order.

5. *People vote.*

Version A. Devisive, reactionary forces are at work in the decadent United States, proving beyond a shadow of a doubt that the masses are so oppressed and exploited under capitalism that they don't know what they want. Imagine 27 million people expressing disapproval of the incumbent administration!

Version B. In the progressive Socialist state of Poland, 99.3% of the eligible voters cast ballots for the single slate of candidates selected for them with the greatest care. This nearly unanimous act of civic responsibility demonstrates overwhelming support for the Premier's progressive policies.

6. *A building is bombed.*

Version A. An unprovoked, war-escalating act of U. S. imperialism against the peaceloving People's Democratic Republic of Vietnam.

Version B. A patriotic act demonstrating that the freedom-loving Vietnamese people want to settle their political future without interference in their internal affairs by American imperialists.

7. *Arms are dispatched.*

Version A. A blatant act of imperialist intervention to prevent the establishment of a democratic and popular government in the Dominican Republic.

Version B. Justified support for a liberation movement which expresses the will of the brave, exploited Congolese people.

8. *A revolt breaks out.*

Version A. A nefarious plot hatched by dissident, counter-revolutionaries and other enemies of the state, supported by imperialist agents and other warmongering elements seeking to overthrow the legitimately constituted government of the peaceloving Socialist state of Hungary.

Version B. A spontaneous uprising against the oppressive, neo-colonial policies of their imperialist exploiters by the freedom-loving people of the Dominican Republic, seeking to determine their historical destiny.

9.   *Planes land.*

Version A. A transparent pretext for rescuing missionaries to cover U. S. imperialist machinations against the Congolese freedom-fighters.

Version B. Material support in the Congolese war of liberation to assist that enslaved, U. S.-puppet state to join the ranks of the truly free nations of the world.

10.   *A UN delegate proposes.*

Version A. A cynical capitalist trick to detract attention from the naked U. S. aggression in Vietnam. An ingenious ruse to infiltrate imperialist agents and saboteurs into the peace-loving Socialist states in the guise of disarmament inspection teams.

Version B. A sensible proposal which only dishonest men can reject. All honest men know that mutual trust must be demonstrated before there can be world peace. If the Soviet Union gives its solemn pledge that it will disarm, the existence of inspection teams only serves to increase international tensions and breed mistrust.

Who Did It? Where?

Note that four of the events — the two versions of the falling leaf, the reading boy, the rioting students and the voting people — are depicted in the context of the "bad capitalist society" and the "good Socialist society", respectively.

Three others — the building bombers, the arms dispatchers and the foreign planes — contract the "aggression" of the "warmongering Imperialist Camp" with the "acts of liberation" of the "freedom-loving Socialist Camp". These acts, it will be observed, took place in the non-Communist world with the result that, if the Communists committed them, they were "right and good", but if we did, they were "wrong and bad".

No. 8 clearly shows that a "revolt" against the government of a "Socialist" state is not the same as a "revolt" within a non-Communist state.

The two versions of the proposal for world disarmament indicate the truly marvelous contrasts that can be created in the Communist lingo, depending upon who makes a proposal.

Discussion of the crying baby contrasts "imperialist aggression" on the one hand with the "peaceful, progressive Socialist society" on the other.

The logic behind the Communist lingo begins to emerge. Who did it? Was it the "good Communists" or the "bad imperialists"? Where did it take place? On "good Socialist" soil or on "bad capitalist" soil? Or did it take place on the soil of the neutral nations, whose governments the Communists try hardest to topple?

"Who did it?" and "Where did it take place?" are basic questions which must be answered before Communist double talkers can give their version of the truth about any event, significant or trivial, that occurs in the world.

It goes without saying that in the Communist lingo the linguistic transmission belt conveys revolutionary messages to Communists everywhere. These messages read: "This is good; support it," or "This is bad; oppose it."

CHAPTER V

IDEOLOGICAL ASSUMPTIONS

> ". . . the patriotic archbishop of Canterbury
> found it advisable —"
> "Found *what?*" said the Duck.
> "Found *it,*" the Mouse replied rather crossly;
> "of course you know what 'it' means."
> "I know what 'it' means well enough when *I*
> find a thing," said the Duck; "it's generally a frog
> or a worm. . ."
>
> —*Alice in Wonderland*

It is now clear how Communists can transmit two
messages at the same time in their double-talk lingo.
The apparent meaning is based on Western concepts
while the revolutionary meaning stems from Marxist-
Leninist concepts. It is equally clear why it is necessary
to know what is behind Marxist-Leninist concepts if
we would translate Communist words into Western
thought.

Linguistic concepts are normally based on unconscious assumptions. What *are* unconscious assumptions,
one may ask?

The dictionary defines an assumption as an "act
taken for granted", and when people are unaware they
are taking something for granted they make unconscious assumptions.

Let us say that the teen-age son wants to borrow the

family car. His father and mother are not home, however, so he can't ask permission. He thinks about it for awhile. Finally, he concludes his parents won't mind, and off he goes in the car. This was a conscious assumption on his part. He thought about it first. But supposing his parents had given him permission to use the car without asking whenever they were not using it. In this case, the teen-ager would not have hesitated; he would simply have jumped into the car and driven off. This illustrates an unconscious assumption. He knew it would be all right without thinking about it.

The classic legal question "When did you stop beating your wife?" contains an unconscious assumption.

"Why don't the American imperialists stop their aggression in Vietnam?" Radio Moscow asks. This rhetorical question contains an unconscious assumption, too. Since the United States is participating in a military activity which is blocking Communist expansion, it is reasonable for them to make the judgment that we are "imperialists" and that what we are doing constitutes "aggression". The revolutionary meanings of these Communist concepts issue logically from the assumption that the United States is the enemy.

Ideological Assumptions

What are the unconscious assumptions which underlie Communist concepts, giving them validity? In the first place, all the assumptions that Communists make are ideological in character, i.e., they are related to the world revolutionary movement. This fact should not come as a surprise, since it was observed in the preceding chapter that all world events can be construed so as to benefit the Cause. In the second place, these ideological assumptions are not always unconscious. Whereas Americans come by their linguistic assumptions naturally, effortlessly and unconsciously, by virtue of a democratic, Judeo-Christian heritage, Communists are taught the foundations upon which their concepts are built.

It is the intention of the Communist Party that the ideological assumptions become unconscious. In fact, the fundamentals of the Marxist-Leninist doctrine are drilled into neophyte Communists with such intensity that these fundamentals do often, indeed, become unconscious assumptions. In general, these fundamentals or assumptions may be divided into two parts: (1) ideological tenets, or what beliefs to hold and (2) ideological action principles, the guidelines for bringing about world revolution.

In passing, the Marxist-Leninist doctrine may be described as Lenin's interpretation of how to bring about the world revolution envisioned by Karl Marx, the "father of Communism".

Ideological tenets

Some of the important Marist-Leninist tenets appear to be the following:

1. Communism (the Socialist system) and Capitalism (the free-enterprise system) are locked together in a titanic class struggle for world hegemony in all areas of human activity.

2. There can be no lasting peace on earth until the class struggle ends in total victory for Communism and all traces of the free-enterprise society have been obliterated.

3. The principal enemy is the United States, the most powerful of the capitalist states.

4. The individual exists to serve the State, i.e., the Communist Party.

5. Lenin himself is regarded as "God", his writings, the "Bible" and the current Party leaders, the chief prophets.

6. World revolution is of supreme importance and other Communist activity is secondary and dependent upon it for valid significance.

7. Language is an ideological tool for advancing the revolutionary cause.

8. The world is viewed as being divided into two parts: (1) Communist-held territory and (2) non-Communist territory. The former is considered to be inviolable and not subject to interference from without. A continuing effort is made, however, to seize non-Communist territory and weaken the enemy wherever and whenever possible (see "class warfare techniques" in the American-style dictionary at the end of this book for methods used).

9. Seized territory must be communized as quickly as conditions permit.

Ideological Action Principles

Some of the guidelines to Communist action against the non-Communist world appear to be as follows:

1. The United States must be constantly attacked and weakened as much and in as many ways as possible.

2. Flexible concepts setting forth the revolutionary version of the truth must be employed, following the Party Line, to present the goodness-rightness of that

which advances the Cause and the badness-wrongness of that which hinders it.

3. The end justifies the means.

4. An illegal act is not a crime *per se;* the real crime is getting caught committing it.

5. Time favors the Cause.

These ideological assumptions — these Marxist-Leninist tenets and precepts — become imbedded in the subconscious of every well-trained Communist. And for those who need reminding, there is always the Party Line, reinforcing them, being constantly transmitted via the Communist lingo.

Perhaps the most portentous ideological assumption, insofar as the West is concerned, is the existence of the unrelenting class struggle against the non-Communist world, in which the United States is the chief adversary. Too many Americans, it seems, fail to recognize the intensity, scope and significance of this struggle. Yet the Communists reaffirm the existence of this drive toward world domination each time they employ the Communist lingo.

Any language is based on a set of invariables, that is, unchanging ideas assumed to be true. Otherwise, language would be unpredictable and consequently without value as a communications medium. The invariables of the Communist lingo are the ideological assumptions listed above. It should not come as a surprise to learn that at least one ideological assumtion undergirds every propaganda utterance. Frequently, more than one can be discovered.

In the *Introduction,* for example, the leader of the Cuban machinegun squad assigned to expropriate the American factory insisted that tire production had decreased because the authorizing decree said so. The facts to the contrary advanced by the plant manager were therefore logically (from the Communist standpoint) called "capitalist lies".

Assumptions: Revolutionary truth points out the badness-wrongness of that which impedes the Cause. In this case, the statistics proving that tire production had increased tended to stand in the way of nationalization of the factory; therefore, they were considered false, bad and wrong — "capitalist lies". Also the end justified the means and the United States was attacked and weakened.

With further reference to Cuba, the fabrications issued by the Revolutionary Government against the United States were, and still are, based on the easily recognizable ideological assumption that we are the enemy. By the same token, the misrepresentations of the Cuban Communist hierarchy concerning itself, its objectives and activities are equally valid — but only if one goes along with the revolutionary system of logic, in which language is used, not to seek truth, but to promote the Cause.

All judgments vocalized in the Communist lingo became plausible in light of the ideological assumptions behind them.

Two Interpretations of Lenin

One can appreciate more fully the depth and intensity of the ideological dispute between Red China and the Soviet Union when it is realized that the Communist Party in both countries maintains that *its* interpretation of Lenin's revolutionary precepts should constitute the Party Line to be followed by Communists in all countries. The Communist "Bible", Lenin's writings, states that armed uprising must be used to bring about world revolution (Red China's position). On the other hand, Lenin also said that a "breathing space" was needed from time to time in the struggle against Capitalism to allow Communists to regroup forces and gain strength. The Russian Communist leaders hold that this breathing space, that is, "peaceful coexistence", is needed before overtly resuming the struggle against the United States.

The two Communist powers do not question the validity of Lenin's revolutionary principles but differ rather on which tactic to employ against Western civilization in the nuclear age.

If the Soviet Union did not consider the United States the enemy, it would not accuse us of "aggression" in Vietnam and elsewhere, a term reserved for enemies. And when a non-Communist state is accused of "aggression" by the Soviet Union, it may consider itself marked for eventual destruction.

VI

WORDS: AUXILIARIES TO SEIZURE AND COMMUNIZATION

"To the Communists, words are tools to achieve effects, not means to communicate in the search for truth."

—Stefan T. Possony

At this point, it may be appropriate to summarize the principal features of the Communist lingo and compare them with the features of an ordinary language.

The Communist lingo expresses those judgments made by Communist Party policy-makers deemed to promote the cause of world revolution. The judgments issue from the ideologically-slanted concepts of what promotes the Cause and what hinders it. Such judgments are considered to contain the revolutionary truth which cannot be present unless the Cause is being advanced. Revolutionary truth, in turn, consists of "facts" that correspond to revolutionary reality, that is, the progress being made in the direction of achieving world revolution. Revolutionary reality is predicated on a series of Marxist-Leninist tenets (setting forth why world revolution is good) and precepts (explaining the most efficacious means of bringing it about).

51

On the other hand, the purpose of any ordinary language, such as English or Japanese, is to communicate the truth. Judgments may be rendered impartially as to what is good and bad, or right and wrong, by individual interpretation of the laws of God and man. The truth appears as absolute in the sense that it exists independently of the effects it may have on people. Some people may not like the truth but they cannot avoid it, unless they wish to take a flight into fancy. (Contrast absolute truth with the Communist brand which is dependent on whether or not the Cause is benefited.) This is because truth conforms to reality, i.e., to the facts as they exist in nature, or as they are created by man. Furthermore, concepts are based on assumptions made unconsciously as to what ideas in general should be.

The manner in which a language is employed does not affect the validity of its structure-function any more than the way money is spent affects its value as a medium of exchange. It is not the fault of the language if its users arrive at inaccurate judgments or even deliberately misrepresent the truth. The point is, people have a choice to express themselves as they see fit in any national language. This is not the case with regard to the Communist lingo wherein only what has been determined by the Communist Party to be true can be expressed.

When the Marxist-Leninist values are superimposed on national languages, two interpretations of statements become possible. Thus any language when vocalized in the Communist lingo can become the vehicle for conveying the revolutionary version of truth in addition to (Western) truth.

The Plan For World Revolution

World revolution is the goal. Marxist-Leninists recognize two related processes as essential to carry out the ambitious project of establishing and maintaining a world-empire of Soviet "republics": (1) the first phase of the Revolution consists of seizing non-Communist territory piece-meal and (2) the second phase is concerned with communizing the territory as it is seized.

Following a plan conceived by Lenin, Communists are busy diminishing Free World holdings wherever and whenever possible, leaving the United States until last. When the "last bastion of Capitalism" is finally isolated and encircled by a ring of Communist or pro-Communist states, it is expected to "fall like an overripe fruit, without a shot having been fired."

First Phase of the Revolution — Seizure

To seize territory, Communists reason, two elements are of prime importance: force and deception. They rely heavily on words of revolutionary import, verbalized in the Communist lingo, to convince the world audience that their use of force (aggression) is something else (liberation). Similarly, their objective for non-Communist countries (Communist dictatorship) is represented by something it is not (freedom, self-determination or independence). Efforts to block Communist expansion are labeled "aggression", and non-Communist governments are described as being oppressive, reactionary, imperialistic, dictatorial, (neo-)Fascist and (neo-)colonial, as appropriate, thereby fully justifying the "wars of national liberation" fomented for the purpose of overthrowing them.

Moreover, to attract support for their immediate objectives, Communists hold out the appealing theory of Marxism; many persons who aid Communism by embracing the Marxist theory do not understand until later that they are being used to help bring about a ruthless dictatorship in their own country. Those who seek to establish "Socialism" in their own country seem to confuse it with the democratic-type Socialism of Sweden or Great Britain. Communists, however, favor any kind of "Socialism", democratic-type or Communist-type, because the more socialist a governments becomes, the closer it gets to Communism. This principle seems to be imperfectly understood, or not understood at all, by the people in non-Communist states.

Second Phase of the Revolution — Communization

Once the "will of the people", i.e., the will of the Communist Party, has been carried out and the government of a non-Communist state overturned, perhaps by a combination of "non-peaceful" (violent and terroristic) and "parliamentary" (legal) means, the second phase of the Revolution begins — communization. However, it is not admitted that the country is being communized, for such admission would cause the United States to withhold technical assistance. Hence, Communist leaders boldly announce they are "building Socialism" or "laying the foundations of Socialism". The pro-Communist government sets about destroying all vestiges of Capitalism. Everything must be nationalized — private property, business, industry and commerce and even people's thoughts. All opposition (enemies of the state) must be "liquidated" (eliminated by execution, imprisonment, exile, etc.) as "counter-revolutionaries".

Under the Communist brand of "Socialism", such concepts as freedom, justice and equality have a special semantic flavor. Comrades are free to do whatever they are told and, so long as they do so, they can enjoy the kind of justice deemed most beneficial to the Communist ruling clique. Any comrade is as equal theoretically as any other comrade, but practically this is not true. Some comrades, or groups of comrades, seem to enjoy more equality than others. The concept of equality appears to be meaningless unless it can be interpreted as the Party sees fit.

So it is evident that the Communist lingo plays an important role in the communization process, too. As can imagined, other ideas are represented so that their meaning may be even opposite to what might be expected. Captive peoples in the "Socialist republics" are asked to accept such Orwellian "truths" as:

Patriotism is "counterrevolutionary activity".
Genocide is "humanitarianism".
Regimentation is "freedom".
Independent thinking is "deviationism".
Why shouldn't two plus two equal five?[1]

[1] In George Orwell's *Nineteen Eighty-four* the protagonist, who lives in a Socialist state, is subjected to physical and mental tortures by a sadistic Party member until he admits that two plus two equals five.

CHAPTER VII

ORIGINS OF THE COMMUNIST LINGO

> "There is no political group in the world which
> understands the value of words as thoroughly as
> do the Communists."
>
> —Natalie Grant,
> Research Institute on the
> Sino-Soviet Bloc, 1961

The double-valued idiom of Communism is an international lingo because (1) it serves the world revolutionary movement and (2) it can be verbalized in any language. The revolutionary significance of such terms as "police brutality", "peaceful coexistence", "liberation movement", "aggression" and "Socialist" pass easily from one national language to another. The Marxist-Leninist implication, for instance, of such a judgment as a "new and aggressive act of U.S. imperialism" is equally clear in Russian, Chinese, Spanish, Arabic or English.

Trained Communists have no difficulty in keeping separate the special meanings of their lingo and the usual sense of words expressed in their native tongue. It appears to be only when they refer to some aspect of Communism that the use of the revolutionary idiom is in order. When they speak with no ideological ax to grind, Communists use the dictionary meanings, just as Americans do in English all the time.

How did this strange but effective duel-edged means of communication originate? The Communist lingo did not, of course, spontaneously evolve as national languages did, paralleling the development and responding to the needs of particular ethnic groups. On the contrary, it was devised — devised to serve an international revolutionary movement and its end-product, a worldwide Communist society. It is a product of the present century.

Lenin's Aesopian Language

In the early 1900's Nikolai Lenin, architect of present Communist policy, was the leader of a small group of Bolshevik revolutionaries in Russia. Because of the rigid censorship, however, the Bolsheviks could not openly call for the overthrow of the Tsarist government and express other radical views in their newspaper and the handbills the circulated. If they had, they would have landed in prison, been exiled to Siberia, or even executed for treason. So Lenin devised what he called an Aesopian language by employing innocuous words which disguised their real meaning. For example, instead of calling for "revolution", Lenin would advocate "reform", and he would refer to the "strict Marxists" instead of the "Bolsheviks".

In this way, Lenin was quite successful in passing along revolutionary messages to his followers without detection.

In 1917 the Tsarist government did indeed fall but Lenin had little to do with it. In fact, he was in Switzerland at the time. However, he managed to re-

turn to Russia and, before the year was out, Lenin
and his group of Bolshevik extremists had maneuvered
the overthrow of the legitimate, democratic government
that had been voted into power. This illegal seizure of
power is known as the "October Revolution". Lenin
became the head of the first Communist-controlled
state, which was given the name of the Union of Soviet
Socialist Republics.

Once they were in power, the Communists discarded
the name "Bolsheviks" as they usually do when a
name has outlived its usefulness, but they no longer had
to employ the Aesopian language. So they reverted to
ordinary terminology in which "terror" meant "terror"
and "world revolution" meant just that. It was frankly
admitted that their ruling clique was a "dictatorship
of the proletariat". Other terms were equally frank.
For a long time, until 1935, in fact, Russian Communist Party leaders called a spade a spade.

Marxism: Communism in Theory

Early in the game Lenin had apparently come to
the conclusion that there were two kinds of Communism: the theoretical and the practical. Idealistic
and dissatisfied elements, principally the workers, of
all nations were urged to become part of an international revolutionary movement. It was purported that
the movement would eventually end in a classless
society in which all men would be free, equal and
happy. Before this could take place, however, Capitalism, the social and economic system held to be responsible for the evils of the world, would have to
be destroyed. Captalism would be replaced, it was
alleged, by a state-controlled "socialist" system, an

intermediate step to the classless society of Communism.

The change from Capitalism to Socialism was destined "historically" to take place on the assumption that the truly harsh lot of the 19th century workers would get worse and worse until they could stand it no more. Then they would spontaneously rise up in country after country against their "exploiting masters" and "throw off their chains". Although the doom of Capitalism in this revolutionary manner was held to be inevitable, Communists were taught that it was their duty to help the "historical" process along as much as possible. This process was the so-called class struggle of the proletariat (workers) against the bourgeoisie (exploiting masters). Here, then, is the essence of Communist theory, or Marxism, after its ideologist, Karl Marx.

Marxism-Leninism: Communism in Practice

Things did not turn out as Marx had predicted. On the contrary, working conditions got better and better and the living standard of the common man improved as the years passed. No spontaneous revolutions occurred, not even at the close of World War I when Germany, at least, was expected to turn Communist. As a matter of fact, the only Communist-controlled state in existence up to the end of the second World War was Soviet Russia, which, as we have seen, did not come into being in the manner Marx had prophesied.

The shrewd Lenin saw in the universal appeal of Marx theoretical Communism a means to achieve absolute power. He conceived of a series of ideological tenets and action principles as guidelines. Lenin converted Marx's class struggle into a ruthless ideological war, world-wide and civilization-deep, against the non-Communist world, with little real regard for the condition of the "exploited workers". Objective: not a utopian classless society but world dictatorship. This, in essense, is practical Communism, or Marxism-Leninism.

Thus the very concept of Communism itself came to refer to diverse ideas: theoretical Marxism and practical Marxism-Leninism.

The Comintern's New Policy

Since 1919 there has been an international organization composed of affiliated national Communist parties and under the leadership of the Russian Communist Party. Its purpose is to facilitate the overthrow of non-Communist governments. In passing, it may be said that although the members of this organization from non-Communist countries are traitors in every respect, in the Communist lingo they are known as "internationalists".

Until 1943 this organization was called the Communist International, or Comintern for short. Since then, Communist activities have been largely carried on by the various national Communist parties under the direction of the Kremlin.

By 1935 Soviet leaders had come to realize that little headway was being made to promote successful revolutions in other countries, even with the assistance of Party members and fellow travelers "from the inside", that is, working against their own country. Orthodox Marxist expressions like "terror", "class warfare", "dictatorship of the proletariat", "revolution" and "labor armies" seemed to be frightening off potential support for the Communist movement. Therefore, a new linguistic policy was adopted.

"The Seventh World Congress of the Communist International laid down the law that Communists no longer should use 'sectarian language'. This means, quite simply, that the Communist message should be couched in terms which have a positive ring in the ears of the audience. Communism must be dressed up as something like democratic liberalism or patriotic nationalism. Offensive and locally unfamiliar terms must be avoided. . . . At the Seventh Comintern Congress . . . the party — the 'world authority' that is — specifically authorized this usage of 'nonsectarian language', which meant that any good Communist would now be able to use language which is not to be found in the classical writing of Marx and Lenin but occurs in Jefferson, Mill — or Jane Addams."[1]

It can be seen that the Comintern decided to develop a double-valued language in imitation of Lenin's Aesopian language. The Marxist-Leninist policy makers evidently reasoned that if professional censors could be fooled by the double meanings of innocent-looking words, how easy it would be to deceive ordinary people who are inclined to accept words at their face value. In 1935, then, Communists began to employ respectable Western labels to disguise their revolutionary activities and concepts and, at the same time, to use derogatory terminology to describe opposition to them.

[1] *Language as a Communist Weapon*, consultation with Dr. Stefan T. Possony, Committee on Un-American Activities, House of Representatives, 86th Congress, 1st Session, U. S. Government Printing Office, Washington, D. C., 1959.

Thus was born the Communist lingo that has been perfected to such a high degree that only after more than three decades does the West seem to be on the point of realizing the revolutionary significance implicit in the hidden, "sectarian" meaning of its double-valued terms.

CHAPTER VIII

"A ROSE BY ANY OTHER NAME. . ."

In 1935 the Communists commenced to perfume themselves semantically with *eau de Cologne* and at the same time to spray non-Communists and all aspects of Capitalism with the essence of sewer water.

Fine Words Mask Evil

There used to be slave-labor camps in the Soviet Union for "enemies of the people", that is, political prisoners. They all disappeared following the adoption of the Comintern's new language policy in 1935. Not physically, of course — only semantically. The same buildings, the same prisoners, the same guards, the same slave-labor and the same inhuman conditions remained as they were before. Only the name changed. They became "corrective labor camps". Doesn't the new label make things seem better?

How about the "People's Democratic Republic of Germany"? After being linguistically perfumed, doesn't the Communist police-state formed from the Soviet Occupation Zone of Germany emerge smelling like a rose?

Fine words mask evil. When the Communists liquidated millions of "uncooperative" farmers in the

Ukraine and on the Chinese mainland in order to establish collective farming, what did they do? Commit murder on a grand scale? No, indeed. They merely instituted "agricultural reform".

And even today when Communists ruthlessly suppress the rights of captive citizens, starve them, torture them, deprive them of the means of livelihood, imprison them in slave-labor camps and forcibly indoctrinate them with false and godless ideas and values, what do they say they are doing? Why, as any well-trained Marxist-Leninist knows, this is "laying the foundations of Socialism" or "building Socialism". Not Communism, mind you, but Socialism.

Castro is busy building Socialism in Cuba today.

Moreover, Marxist-Leninist "premiers" or "presidents" in such African states as Algeria and Tanzania freely admit that they, too, are building Socialism.

And what are those "fraternal parties" that Communist leaders talk about? Are they shindigs thrown by the Elks, Kiwanis or Knights of Columbus? They are decidedly not. They are Communist and pro-Communist groups and organizations.

Communists are quite sensitive to the emotional impact that words have on people. Even the word, Communism, which is unpleasant to the Western ear (although since we began "coexisting peacefully" with the Soviet Union, it seems to be getting more and more respectable — except the Red Chinese brand) may be replaced by more acceptable terms such as "Socialism", "anti-Fascism", "anti-imperialism" and "anti-colonialism".

Respectability Through Labels

When the political warfare tactics so demand, Communists may refer to themselves and their followers as "the forces of peace", "the forces of freedom", "the forces of progress", "the forces of reason" or "the forces of" — practically anything else that is good and respectable. Then again, Communist revolutionaries — traitors to their own country — may be designated as "freedom fighters" or "partisans of peace".

In Havana, the processing agency for Cuba's terrorist trainees, who export revolution to other Latin American countries, is known as the "Institute of People's Friendship".

Note the positive ring to the name of the following American organizations:

League for Common Sense
Michigan Council for Peace
People's Drama, Inc.
Voice of Freedom Committee
Committee for the Negro in the Arts
American Patriots, Inc.
National Blue Star Mothers of America

These titles were taken at random from the Attorney General's List of Subversive Organizations. The latest U.S. Government Guide to Subversive Organizations (House Document No. 398, 87th Congress, 2nd Session) lists 663 organizations or projects and 122 publications cited as Communist or Communist front by Federal agencies and 155 organizations and 25 publications cited as Communist or Communist front by state or territorial investigating committees. Many of the organizations have names that suggest home, mother and country. Yet these organizations have been investigated by the FBI and other security agencies and found to be inimical to the interests and welfare of the nation. Their common purpose: to help overthrow the United States Government.

The number of high-sounding labels Communists use to disguise themselves and their revolutionary activities seems to have no limit.

Making the West Sound Bad

But what about us? Since the Communists can make words mean anything they choose to, how does the West smell after being verbally sprayed with Drain Pipe No. 5? Pretty bad, naturally. A few examples will serve to illustrate.

Our Federal Bureau of Investigation does an excellent job in uncovering Communist skullduggery and espionage. What is the FBI called in the Communist lingo? The "American Gestapo".

What label do Communists apply to the hearings of the Committee on Un-American Activities, which has issued dozens of publications exposing various aspects of Communism? Since much of the Committee's information is obtained from personal testimony, Communists call Committee hearings "Star Chamber proceedings", suggesting the infamous Star Chamber of medieval England in which secrecy and torture were used.

Two labels of fairly recent vintage favored by Communist propagandists are "police brutality" and "escalation". Whenever law enforcement officers are compelled to use force to control or disperse a riot or a demonstration that has gotten out of hand, the cry of "police brutality" is raised. Early in 1965 the term "escalation" began to be widely used in connection with increased military activity to cope with increased

Communist pressures in South Vietnam. The implication is that the United States is deliberately and unjustifiably expanding the war.

For other depreciatory labels describing the United States and things and persons American, see the list of "bad words" in the next section.

"Good Words" and "Bad Words"

Because the United States is the enemy it is proper for Communists to call us all the bad names they can think of. By the same token, by virtue of being Communists, they themselves are the recipients of all the good names. The purpose of this "good-name-bad-name" technique is to spread misunderstanding throughout the world. It would be interesting to know how many people on this globe hate and misunderstand the United States because of Communist propaganda and how many have been duped into believing that Communism is a good thing for the same reason.

Two lists follow. One contains some of the "bad words" Communists use to describe the American people, our policies, institutions and activities.[1] The other consists of the "good words" which they apply to themselves.

"BAD WORDS"	"GOOD WORDS"
aggression	self-defense
aggressors	liberators

[1] The "bad words" are also applied to any non-Communists, regardless of nationality, when appropriate, and to any aspect of Capitalism in any state. They are used more frequently in the political and propaganda warfare against the United States which alone stands in the way of Soviet world conquest.

anti-moral	moral
bourgeois	popular; proletarian
bourgeois ideologists	Soviet policy makers
bourgeois international law	modern international law
bourgeois landlords	Socialist leaders
bourgeois governments	Socialist governments
Capitalism	Socialism
chauvinists	internationalists
colonialism	anti-colonialism; self-determination
colonial power	Socialist power
criminal discrimination	racial equality
decadent	progressive
dishonest men	honest men
dollar imperialism	ruble aid
enemies of peace	Soviet friendship
exploiters	liberators
Fascism	anti-Fascism; democracy
Fascist bosses	Socialist leaders
feudal lords	Socialist leaders
forces of reaction, oppression, etc.	forces of progress, freedom, peace, reason, etc.
foreign policy myths	foreign policy realities
Gestapo methods	Soviet law enforcement
gorillas	partisans (of peace)
imperialism	Socialism; liberation
Imperialist Camp	Socialist Camp
imperialist murderers	freedom fighters
intellectual dishonesty	intellectual honesty
intervention	liberation
lackeys of imperialism, of the capitalist police-state, Wall Street, etc.	fraternal parties; peace-loving states
madmen	responsible leaders

manhaters	peacelovers
neo-Colonialism	Soviet technical assistance
oppressors	liberators
paper tiger	Chinese military might
peacehating	peace-loving
persecution	will of the people; Soviet justice
police brutality	Soviet law enforcement
police state	peoples democratic republic
political prisoners	criminals; enemies of the state
racial discrimination	racial equality
reactionary	progressive
repressive	popular
stool-pigeons	progressive elements
Storm Trooper tactics	Soviet law enforcement
The Establishment	Soviet customs and institutions
Uncle Toms	progressive elements
unjust wars	just wars
vultures of Wall Street	leaders of the workers' state
warmongering	peace-loving
wars of aggression	wars of liberation
wildmen	responsible leaders
Yankee imperialism	international cooperation

The two lists are not exhaustive, of course, and new terms are constantly being invented, but they do illustrate how Communist propaganda slants things in favor of Communism and against the free-enterprise system. All the "good" and "bad" words have double meanings when expressed in the Communist lingo, which tends to cause confusion and controversy on the part of Americans who see and hear them. And the confusion and controversy are compounded because there is usually some element of truth in Communist claims. More often than not, Americans become so busy explaining the small truthful part of some Communist allegation that they lose sight of the its real purpose and significance — the United States is bad and must be constantly attacked while the Soviet Union is good and must constantly be defended.

Communist spokesmen have no difficulty in selecting which list to choose from in a given situation. If we did it, or they are referring to us, "bad words" are automatically selected. If they did it, or they are referring to themselves, "good words" are in order. Naturally the more virulent expressions are employed during the Cold War phase of the international climate. The name-calling is toned down appropriately so long as the Communists are "peacefully coexisting" with the United States.

The King Can Do No Wrong

The "bad words" are rarely used by one Communist state to refer to another Communist state, even in such an acrimonious ideological dispute as now considered to exist between Red China and the Soviet Union. Marxist-Leninist leaders in both states realize that a change of Party leadership in either state could bring the dispute to an abrupt end, i.e., if Mao Tse-Tung should be replaced by a Chinese leader who favored "peaceful coexistence", the current Soviet line.

On the other hand, the "good words" can never be applied to the United States and its activities, *unless what we do benefits the Cause* in some way that may not be clear to us at the time. And even then, great care must be exercised lest the impression be given that the enemy Capitalist system is being praised.

One is reminded of the European kings in the Middle Ages who ruled by "divine right" and could therefore do no wrong. For nowadays, King Communism can do no wrong while that notorious villain, the United States, can do nothing right!

CHAPTER IX

INTERNATIONAL POLITICAL CLIMATES

"During the years since 1946, when the iron curtain clanked down, relations between the United States and the Soviet Union have traced the path of the pendulum. The deliberate Soviet policy has been to 'talk tough' for a time, then to withdraw for awhile and give the impression that the two countries might work out their differences. These pulsations are reflected in the polls. Each time the Soviets lower the cold war temperature a few degrees, a substantial number of Americans indicate to the pollsters that they believe the nation might be at war within six months. Yet as soon as the Communists permit a moderating breeze to flow across the world, citizens seem to forget their apprehensions, lapse into apathy, and fail to support all-out defensive or economic-aid measures that might require sacrifices in their standards of living."

—*The American Political Process*
Charles R. Adrian and Charles Press
(McGraw Hill Book Company
New York, N.Y., 1965)

"Sammy," asks Ivan, "will you lend me your skates? I want to go skating this afternoon and mine are broken."

"You've got a lot of nerve," retorts Sammy, "asking to borrow my skates after all those dirty names you've been calling me. And that's not all, either. You've been telling it all around that you and your gang are going to beat up on me the first time you catch me alone. No siree, you don't get *my* skates, Ivan. We're mad at each other."

"Aw, come on, Sammy," coaxes Ivan, "you know I didn't mean anything. I was just kidding. Names can't hurt you. You know that. And besides, if my gang beats up on you, then your gang will beat up on me the first chance *they* get. Come on, Sammy, let's make up. Lend me your skates. I'll give you that whistle of mine you've always wanted if you do."

So the two boys become friends again. Ivan gets to use the skates and Sammy gets the whistle.

This changeabout in attitude was accomplished with words.

The principle involved is that if you want something from your enemy, offer him something *he* wants and pretend to make up with him. After you've gotten what you want from him, you can discontinue the pretense of friendship and openly resume your enmity. It works even better if your enemy happens to be a nice guy who would willingly be your friend for keeps if you only gave him half a chance.

The principle applies not only to small boys and their neighborhood gangs but also to nations grouped together in power blocs, such as the United States and its Free World allies and the Soviet Union and its satellites. When applied to nations grouped together in power blocs, the attitudes of friendliness and unfriendliness are known as international political climates. The unfriendly climate is called the Cold War and the friendly climate is called "peaceful coexistence".

The Cold War and "Peaceful Coexistence"

During the Cold War period the Communists appear bellicose, threatening and uncooperative. This is the time for the virulent epithet and the challenge — the threat to level Bonn, Rome and Paris; and the exaggeration of Soviet military might in an attempt to impress the neutral nations — to persuade through intimidation. The undeveloped nations of Asia, the Middle East, Africa and Latin America are simultaneously the pawns and the prizes in the world struggle between the willing "Socialist Camp" and the reluctant "Imperialist Camp". Within the United States, laws are tightened against Communist activity, Communism is a dirty word and people fear that a nuclear holocaust may be in the offing.

During the counterpart "peaceful coexistence" phase, the Communists show themselves as relatively restrained in their propaganda and seemingly cooperative with the West. This is the time of the "Spirit of Camp David" or the "Spirit of Hollybush", the time to try again to gain some advantages by negotiating treaties, the time to bolster the sagging economies of the Socialist countries through Western technical assistance and trade agreements, the time for bigwig Marxist-Leninists to visit non-Communist countries, the time for allowing some controlled peeps behind the Iron Curtain — in short, a time for the showing of the smiling face of "Big Brother".

Within the United States, Communists operate openly, often defiantly, nibbling away at the foundations of the nation under the protective mantle of free speech. There is renewed agitation for abolishing the "watchdog committees" of government — the House

Committee on Un-American Activities and the Senate Internal Security Subcommittee — and for doing away with loyalty oaths of all kinds. Verbal brickbats are hurled at the FBI and real ones at the police. Communist front groups spring up like mushrooms. Communists exploit every conceivable weakness of the free-enterprise society, from participating in racial disturbances to using the civil-rights movements as a justification for a "Black Revolution". U.S. foreign policy in Vietnam and elsewhere is viciously attacked. On college campuses, student groups of the so-called New Left oppose all forms of authority. Sincere Americans come to believe in the fanciful "convergence theory", which hold that since Communism seemingly is becoming more capitalistic and Capitalism is becoming more socialistic the two systems will one day merge into a single system, shucking off the disadvantages and retaining the advantages of both. Communism become a respectable word to describe a relatively harmless political theory held by the Russians, but it retains the familiar sinister connotation of "world revolution" when applied to Red China.

In a word, many Americans are convinced that the Soviet leopard has changed his spots for good. This is "peaceful coexistence".

How Peaceful is "Peaceful Coexistence"?

Let us take a closer look at the term, "peaceful coexistence", and see how peaceful it really is. How do Communists interpret it? In his pamphlet, *Language as a Communist Weapon,* Dr. Possony has this to say about the concept of coexistence when interpreted from the revolutionary point of view:

"The bone 'coexists' with the dog; the rope 'coexists' with the man who is hanged; bacilli 'coexist' with your body. Coexistence is a transitory matter of fact. . . . For the time being, the Soviet Union cannot stop co-existing with non-Communist nations. . . . Coexistence also is a slogan to lull non-Communists to sleep and to induce economic and political support for the Soviet Union. It specifically does *not* mean that any Communists ought to be prepared to coexist with the capitalist system till the end of the world. Essentially, the term is a deception to convey the impression that the world revolution has been called off."

In one revolutionary sense, "peaceful" means "not opposing Communist aims". "Peaceful coexistence", when translated from the Communist lingo, emerges as a period of time during which the West, believing that the Soviet Union has given up its goal of world domina-tion, actually assists in bringing about its own down-fall — in an international climate of seeming peace.

In 1964 the Standing Committee on Education Against Communism of the American Bar Association published a heavily documented study. Its title is *Peaceful Coexistence — A Communist Blueprint for Victory*. In this excellent treatise are to be found numerous quotations from Communist sources ex-plaining why "peaceful coexistence" is considered to be a Communist stratagem to overthrow the United States.

Lest the impression be given that the Soviet Union has a monoply on this clever subterfuge, it should be recalled that Red China coexisted with Tibet for a short time before feeling strong enough (1951) to ab-sorb that country into its colonial empire. It is there-fore not inconceivable that Red China might some day find itself in need of a "breathing space" in its struggle against the United States. If Mao Tse-Tung's "cultural revolution" should fail and the "Khrushchev revisionists", i.e., Party members who advocate temporary "peaceful coexistence" with the West, should come to power, this could very well be the case. In this event, the Soviet-Red Chinese ideological differences could be readily patched up and united; they could give their full attention to disposing of their common enemy, the United States.

By the same token, however, the present leaders of the Soviet Union, or their successors, might find it advantageous to revert to the Cold War at some future date.

In its revolutionary sense, then, "peaceful coexistence" is decidedly not a "normalization of relations" between East and West, as many Western statesmen seem to think.

"How did we come to coexist so peacefully with the Soviet Union?" one may be tempted to ask. The next chapter will tell how we got "peaceful coexistence" in three months and who was responsible for it.

CHAPTER X

"PEACEFUL COEXISTENCE"
IN THREE MONTHS

> "The basic Communist strategy in 1952 re-
> nounced the inevitability of world war III. World
> conquest without war, which is called coexist-
> ence, became their basic strategy."
>
> —Dr. Fred C. Schwartz

On July 1, 1963 Soviet Premier Nikita Khrushchev made a speech in East Berlin. During the course of that speech he angrily declared that West Germany would "burn first" if the West dared to start a war with the mighty Soviet Union — a typical Cold War threat.

Less than three months later, the United States and the Soviet Union, the erstwhile enemies, were coexisting together peacefully. In fact, they are coexisting so peacefully that one of the highest officials of the U.S. government felt obliged to observe that "there are signs the Russians are beginning to modify their long-range objective of dominating the world". By that time, several other noteworthy things had happened:

(1) We had negotiated a treaty with the Soviet Union;

(2) A high U.S. official had denied that treaties with the Communists are worthless;

(3) We had invited the Russians to join us in an expedition to the moon;

(4) We were preparing to sell wheat to the Soviet bloc, a prelude to a brisk East-West trade; and

(5) We were beginning to believe that there are really two major brands of Communism: (a) the relatively harmless kind advocated by the "peacefully coexisting" Soviet bloc states and (b) the dangerous kind espoused by the militant Red Chinese.

As an indication of how completely the American attitude toward the Soviet Union was reversed in 1963, we are indebted to two public opinion polls taken that year. In the Spring, when the Cold War was raging, a Scripps-Howard pollster, Samuel Lubell, reported that 75% of the people interviewed considered the struggle with Russia to be the No. 1 problem facing the nation. In October, however, a similar poll revealed that only 25% of the people held the Soviet Union to be this country's major problem. At that time, of course, we were "peacefully coexisting" with the Soviet Union.

How Khrushchev did it

Did this remarkably swift and radical change in international relations and attitudes "just happen", or was it planned?

It is suggested that the whole thing was engineered and executed by Soviet Premier Khrushchev with little more than words — double-talk Communist words, it goes without saying.

The thesis is advanced that the world political climate is manipulated from Moscow[1] and that the Free

[1] And also from Peking since 1963 by virtue of the Soviet-Red Chinese ideological split.

World reacts in a relatively friendly or unfriendly fashion toward the Soviet Union in particular and Communism in general, depending upon whether the climate is of the "peaceful coexistence" variety or its alternating phase, the Cold War. Purpose: to promote the unchanging objective of world revolution.

In defense of this thesis, 19 newspaper headlines are presented. These headlines, which appeared in American newspapers during the period July 2 - September 26, 1963, depict the sequence of Khrushchev's successful manipulations of the world political climate:

July 2	RUSS OFFERS SWAP: WEST'S N-BAN FOR NONAGGRESSION PACT
July 16	NIKITA OPENS TEST BAN PARLEY IN JOVIAL MOOD
July 21	IS THE COLD WAR DUE FOR A THAW?
July 25	NIKITA URGES AFRICA BE MADE NUCLEAR-FREE
July 26	KHRUSHCHEV HOPEFUL OF FULL DISARMAMENT
July 27	NUCLEAR TEST BAN TREATY COULD BE BIG TURNING POINT
July 27	NIKITA URGES PEACE PACT
Aug. 1	TEST BAN TREATY IS CRUCIAL FIRST STEP
Aug. 2	KHRUSHCHEV SAID EAGER TO STOP INDIA-CHINA WAR
Aug. 13	HARRIMAN DECRIES CHARGE RED PACTS ARE WORTHLESS
Aug. 31	RED QUIZ U. S. GOLF COURSE BUILDING PLANS
Sept. 1	HINTS APPEAR OF MAJOR SOVIET POLICY SHIFT
Sept. 4	KHRUSHCHEV, TITO AGREEMENT SEEN PRODUCT OF RED CHANGE
Sept. 20	RUSK TO DISCUSS U. S.-RUSSIA TRADE

Sept. 21 PRESIDENT INVITES RUSSIANS TO JOIN MOON EXPEDITION

Sept. 25 RUSK SLATES TALKS WITH GROMYKO

Sept. 25 U. S. GRAIN TRADERS SAID WORKING ON RUSSIAN DEAL

Sept. 25 CZECHS WILLING TO BUY WHEAT, AIDE TELLS RUSK

Sept. 26 McNAMARA BELIEVES NIK MODIFYING GOAL

A cursory study of the headlines will reveal that Khrushchev applied the principle alluded to in the previous chapter: ". . . if you want something from your enemy, offer him something *he* wants and pretend to be friends with him."

It will be recalled that Ivan gave his enemy, Sammy, a whistle in exchange for the loan of Sammy's skates. And the two boys became "friends".

The Soviet Union gave the United States a "treaty" and the promise of peace in exchange for "peaceful coexistence".

Khruschev's formula for ushering in "peaceful co-existence" can be detected by a further analysis of the newspaper headlines: appear cooperative in dealings with the West (advocate treaties and trade); urge that peaceful steps be taken in international matters (make Africa nuclear-free and work toward full disarmament) and come out in favor of peace (stop the India-Chinese war).

Lest we forget: the key terms in Khrushchev's formula also have revolutionary meanings. *Cooperation, treaties, trade, peaceful steps, disarmament* and *peace* should be read as Soviet-type cooperation, Soviet-type treaties, etc.

Khrushchev Tipped His Hand

Words are indeed power-tools in Communist political warfare, cheap and effective in changing attitudes. The double-valued Communist lingo always reveals Communist plans, however, if we can but interpret the words in the revolutionary sense — the one not intended for us.

How did Krushchev tip his hand? Let's see.

During the course of the test ban treaty negotiations (July 1963), the Soviet Premier was reported by the Russian Communist news agency, *Tass,* as saying in a program beamed to Africa that "East-West agreement on a nuclear test ban could effect a 'radical change' toward bettering the world climate". Khrushchev was quoted as saying, "We shall go on doing everything to ease international tensions, to consolidate peace by implementing the principle of peaceful coexistence among states."

East-West agreement, bettering the world climate, easing international tensions, consolidating peace and *peaceful coexistence.*

Didn't Khrushchev's words sound fine after years of Soviet threats and insults during the Cold War years, and especially after the Cuban missile crisis the preceding year which brought the United States to the brink of war? Weren't these fine words just what the tension-weary West had been longing to hear?

According to their dictionary meaning, yes.

But their revolutionary import is quite different.

In the Communist lexicon, an "agreement" is, of course, as Lenin pointed out, a means of gaining strength. Any treaty, nuclear or otherwise, will be honored by the Communists only so long as it is advantageous to do so. Then it will be cynically abrogated, as the scores of treaties broken by the Soviet Union in the past mutely testify.

When Khrushchev told the African nations that a nuclear test ban "could effect a 'radical turn' toward bettering the world climate", listening Communists everywhere understood that the world climate for indirect aggression would become markedly more advantageous if the treaty materialized.

It has already been noted that according to revolutionary logic "international tensions", being always caused by non-Communist states, can be eased only by their giving in to the Soviet Union. Khrushchev "eased" "international tensions" by getting the United States to "agree" to a "treaty", which the Soviet Union obviously desired very much. If, of course, we had refused to have any part of the treaty, international tensions would have been increased.

As if his revolutionary message to Africa were not clear enough, the double-talking Communist leader added that "peace" would be consolidated by implementing the principle of "peaceful coexistence" among states. As previously pointed out, in such a context, "peace" means Western policy favorable to Communist aims. The Communist conception of "peaceful coexistence" needs no further explanation.

Translated from the Communist lingo, here is what Khrushchev told his Communist audience: "The Soviet Union will go on duping the West and persuading the United States to bend to Communist will, thus making it easier for us to implement our principle of conquering states by indirect aggression in an atmosphere of peace."

Marxist-Leninist listeners got the message: No more Cold War. Until further instructions from the Soviet Communist Party, it's "peaceful coexistence".

Khrushchev tipped his hand but apparently the West was too busy heaving a sigh of relief that the Cold War was over to see that he held four aces.

"A Mature and Fruitful Line"

The architect of "peaceful coexistence" has passed into oblivion. In the Communist jargon, he is considered to be an "unperson"; that is, for the purpose of Soviet history, he did not exist. And he is seldom heard from these days, except when he can be useful to the Cause, i.e., public appearances now and then (Communism allegedly has changed, so that ousted Communist leaders are retired pretty much as they are in any other country) or perhaps serving as the subject of a television documentary (1967) which many Americans thought was out-and-out Communist propaganda, regardless of the intent of the U.S. television program producer.

But what was Khrushchev's opinion of "peaceful coexistence" when he was a "person"? On December 30, 1963 when it already appeared that the West intended to coexist peacefully as long as the Soviet Union might wish, he was quoted as saying that such "peaceful cooperation" was "a weapon more perfect than ballistic missiles or nuclear submarines".

And what did his successors in the Kremlin have to say about Khrushchev's "weapon" following his ouster from power less than a year later? A UPI despatch datelined Moscow December 20, 1964 quoted *Pravda,* another Russian Communist news organ, as follows:

"This [peaceful coexistence] was a mature and fruitful line which deeply accelerated contemporary social developments. . ."

Translated from the Communist lingo, the statement reads: "The time-schedule for the downfall of the United States was stepped up considerably. . ."

Is it any wonder that the "peaceful coexistence" stratagem was reaffirmed as the official policy of the Soviet Union? One cannot help wondering: Would U.S. policy-makers be quite so eager to "build bridges" of trade and cooperation with the Soviet Union if they were thoroughly grounded in the basics of the Communist lingo?

CHAPTER XI

THE STATUS QUO — COMMUNIST STYLE

"Oh looky, Ivan," shouts Sammy excitedly, running up to his new friend, "look what I got! A whole dollar!"

"Humph," grunts Ivan without looking up from his game of mumbly-peg, "where'd you get it?"

"My Dad gave it to me for cutting the grass," replies Sammy, still out of breath; "Wanna see the picture of George Washington on it?"

Ivan ignores the proffered bill. "I'll say I don't," he retorts angrily. "I don't want to see anything your mean old man had anything to do with. I know he's boss down at the glass works. I've heard how he bullies everybody around. They should all get together and kick him out, that's what they should, and take over the plant. By rights, it's theirs. That's what *my* Dad says. And that's why I don't want to see your old capitalistic dollar."

Sammy looks dejectedly at the bill in his hand, wondering what has gotten into his erstwhile friend.

Suddenly Ivan reaches out, snatches the money away from Sammy and thrusts it into his pants pocket. Then, getting to his feet, both fists clenched menacingly, he glares at his suprised playmate. "It's mine," he announces challengingly; "you have no right to it."

This fanciful incident of childhood illustrates in a

simple manner how Communist states establish the *status quo ante bellum,* or *status quo* for short. In the parlance of international law the *status quo* means the way things were before the war. In this instance, the *status quo* before the fight between the two boys broke out could be either (1) when Sammy had possession of his dollar or (2) after Ivan seized it. The former may be considered the Western viewpoint and the latter, the Communist. Let us pursue the matter from Ivan's (the Communist) viewpoint and we shall see the logic behind the Communist interpretation of such terms as provocation, self-defense, aggression, atrocity, escalation, negotiations, peaceful settlement and controversial.

Sammy doubles up his fists, too, and it looks as if he were determined to recover his dollar by force. Seeing this, Ivan warns, "Don't you go picking a fight with me (provocation) or you'll wish you hadn't!" (That is, Ivan will fight back vigorously in self-defense.) Sammy hauls off and lets Ivan have one, whereupon Ivan shouts, *"You* started it!" (Aggression). They lock arms and tumble to the ground with Ivan on top; he starts beating Sammy's head against a rock. (Justified self-defense). Then Sammy rolls Ivan over on his back and, sitting astride the other boy's chest, begins to pummel him in the face with both fists. "You're not fighting fair," Ivan protests, "hitting a guy when he's down. (Atrocity). You're making a big fight out of this!" (Escalation).

The scuffle continues for several minutes. Some other boys gather around to watch. They ask, "Who started it?" Sammy and Ivan pause a moment, panting, and then pointing to each other, exclaim simultaneous-

ly, *"He* did!" Not knowing which to believe, the on-
lookers shrug their shoulders and walk away, muttering
under their breath, "What a mixed-up deal! Nobody
can tell who started it. (Controversial). Let's stay
out of it!"

After a while, the two boys get tired and Ivan says,
"We aren't getting anywhere this way. Let's stop
fighting and talk about who should get the dollar."
(Negotiations and peaceful settlement).

It is repeated that insofar as Ivan is concerened,
the *status quo* to which they should return for discussion, the point at which subsequent actions are
judged, is immediately *after* he took Sammy's dollar.
As with the Communists when they negotiate, Ivan has
nothing to lose, and the best Sammy can hope for is
to break even on the deal — like non-Communists
when they negotiate with Communists.

From Ivan's point of view, Sammy started the fight.
Ivan merely defended himself. If Sammy, however,
had "viewed the matter sensibly", that is, let Ivan keep
the dollar, there would have been no trouble. Later
on during the scuffle, fearing he might lose the fight
(and the money), Ivan was willing to negotiate to see
who was entitled to keep Sammy's dollar. Unless he
got to keep it, he would not consider the settlement
to be a peaceful one.

Thus, the *status quo,* in its revolutionary sense, is
the key to understanding many terms used by Communists in their class struggle with nations of the Free
World. *Status quo* appears to have two related meanings in the Communist lingo, one general and one
specific. In his book, *Peace With Russia?* (Simon and
Schuster, N.Y., 1959), Ambassador Averell Harriman

told of a talk he had had with Soviet Premier Khrushchev during a 1959 visit to Russia, which reveals both meanings. In Harriman's words:

"While he insisted that the Soviet Union only wanted to preserve the status quo, he made it very clear that his idea of the status quo was not the preservation of existing boundaries and balances. An essential element of the world's status today, as Khrushchev sees it, is the Communist march toward world domination. Anything that opposes Communism on the march he considers as altering the status quo and is therefore an act of aggression."

This is the revolutionary conception of the generic significance of *status quo* — Communism on the march. Ambassador Harriman continued, illustrating how the concept is applied in specific cases:

"When the United States sent a small military training group to Laos, *Pravda* blatantly charged that the United States was committing an act of aggression by helping the Laotians defend themselves against a Communist invasion from North Vietnam."

It is now clear that "aggression" disturbs the Communist-determined *status quo* when these two terms are considered in their revolutionary sense. To translate into Western thought: A non-Communist state which defends itself against Communist aggression impedes the march toward domination and, in Communist eyes, this non-Communist self-defense is *ipso facto* deemed "aggression".

The Israeli-Arab War

During and after the Israeli blitzkrieg victory over the Arab states in early June 1967, Communist and

Arab spokesmen in the United Nation and elsewhere tirelessly repeated charges of Israeli aggression. Israel, of course, *was* guilty of aggression in the Communist sense of defending itself against threatened annihilation. But how did Israel's action satisfy the revolutionary definition after the strategic "status quo" had been set up? To find out, it is patently necessary to see what prior illegal action had been taken against Israel.

On May 22, 1967 President Gamal Abdel Nasser announced that Egyptian forces had imposed a blockade against Israeli shipping to the Red Sea through the Gulf of Aqaba. "The Israeli flag shall not go through the Gulf of Aqaba," Nasser declared. "Our sovereignty over the entrance to the gulf cannot be disputed. If Israel wishes to threaten war, we tell her: 'You are welcome.' "

Here we have a situation analagous to Ivan's grabbing Sammy's dollar, thus establishing the *status quo* from which all ensuing actions would be judged.

A glance at the map reveals that the waters of the Gulf of Aqaba wash on the shores of not only Egypt, but Israel, Jordan and Saudi Arabia as well, thus clearly constituting an international waterway. Having committed a provocative, illegal act, by violating an accepted norm of international law, Nasser then proceeded to challenge Israel to use the gulf. If Israel had insisted on exercising its right as a sovereign state and had tried to send one of its ships through, the Arab world, rendering a Communist-type judgment, could have appropriately retaliated against the "provocation" and "aggression" by "defending itself"!

How did the Soviet Union, representing the Communist world, view the situation? How did it consider the position of Israel following the establishment of the "status quo"? Remember at this time, three war-contributing steps had been taken: (1) the ill-advised (from the Western point of view) withdrawal of the UN peace-keeping force from this Middle East hot spot; (2) the massing of overwhelming numbers of Soviet-equipped troops on tiny Israel's borders, plus Arab threats to destroy Israel; and (3) the illegal and war-provoking act of sealing off an international waterway vital to Israeli shipping. How? Kremlin spokesmen made it quite clear that the Soviet Union regarded Israel as the "potential aggressor". In other words, if the small Jewish state resisted with force the Arab encirclement and the closing of the Gulf of Aqaba, such resistance would be deemed "aggression" and dealt with accordingly. In keeping with this line of thought, the entire Communist world would be morally justified in giving all possible assistance to the Arab states to help themselves in their "self-defense" against Israeli "aggression".

Now the stage was set. . .

The moment Israel launched its lightening, defensive attack against the Arabs, all the charges flowing from this change in this general "status quo" (i.e., an attempt to resist Communist-supported aggression) and the specific, tactical "status quo" (i.e., after Israel was surrounded and challenged to use the Gulf of Aqaba) became applicable. It was thus in keeping with Communist logic to accuse Israel of breach of peace, aggression, starting a war, unprovoked attack, escalating international tensions, committing atrocities, and so on.

When, however, it soon became evident that the Arab states were faced with a resounding defeat, the tune was changed and the cry immediately went up for a cease-fire, a truce, a peaceful settlement — anything to bring this "unjust war" to a halt.

As a consequence, attempts were made in the UN by the Communist/Arab bloc to have Israel condemned as the aggressor in the eyes of "world opinion", which is another way of saying that they tried to convince the non-Communist world that the Communist version of the events in the Middle East was the one that corresponded to the facts. Because people in the West in general, and Western statesmen and diplomats in particular, apparently do not fully appreciate the significance of the double-valued Communist lingo, the result is confusion and controversy with regard to almost any activity engaged in by the Communists. Hence, many non-Communist leaders tended to take the Communist accusation of "Israeli aggression" with more seriousness than perhaps it really deserved.

With Israeli troops occupying Egyptian soil up to the east bank of the Suez Canel as well as parts of Syria and Jordan, the tactical *status quo* necessarily had to undergo modification. Accordingly, the Soviet/Arab demands now made were that Israel return to her boundaries existing prior to the six-day war. In the meantime, President Nasser publicly vowed that the struggle would go on, meaning that future actions of Israel and other "imperialist" powers would continue to be evaluated from the vantage point of the long-range or general *status quo* — the Communists march toward world domination.

In Vietnam the Communist-established *status quo* is the effort to overthrow the Saigon government. All efforts to change this status are therefore, following Khrushchev's definition, acts of aggression and all Communists states feel it their moral duty to help their ideological brothers defend themselves.

In 1965 the revolutionary *status quo* in the Dominican Republic was an attempted takeover of the government, thwarted by U.S. "intervention" and "aggression".

As can be seen, with this type of *status quo,* the defendents become the aggressors and the aggressors, the defenders. No wonder "world opinion" cannot make up its collective mind as to who is doing what to whom on the international scene!

CHAPTER XII

THE VERBAL JUNGLES OF VIETNAM

> "For the communist, freedom, democracy, equality, fraternity and, above all, peace can come only when communism is firmly established throughout the world. Whatever forces oppose communism, they are by their very nature reactionary, undemocratic, fascist, anti-popular and repressive. When we study the communist viewpoint, we must consider it in terms of these double values."
>
> —*Communist Propaganda Techniques* by
> John C. Clews
> (Frederick A. Praeger, Publishers
> New York-Washington, 1964)

The situation in Vietnam is a confusing, controversial one and the confusion and controversy seem to be compounded by the widespread acceptance of the Communist interpretation of what is really happening in that unhappy, war-torn land. Consequently, it is pertinent to see how the representation of events in the revolutionary idiom promotes Communist objectives. First, let us consider how "peace" can be brought about.

Communist Formula for "Peace"

A. There will be peace in Vietnam when the southern part is incorporated in the northern part under Communist rule.

B. The U.S. military presence in Vietnam prevents peace.

C. Therefore, the U.S. troops should leave.

Thus the Communist formula for their kind of peace is basically a simple one. In their propaganda pitch to convince "world opinion" that their view is the proper one, Communist spokesmen everywhere dress up the formula in a sophisticated, appealing way by vocalizing it in their double-valued lingo. It runs something like this:

"*International tensions* could be easily *reduced* in Vietnam and a *peaceful settlement* to the war reached quickly. The United States could bring this about unilaterally by ending its *aggression* and withdrawing its troops from Southeast Asia. The dispute could then be settled *peacefully* through *negotiations*. An *agreement* could be reached whereby a *coalition government,* representing all dissident elements, would be formed. *Free elections* would be held *in due time.* Eventually, the North and South would be *reunited* under a *democratic* government. Is it not *just* for the Vietnamese *people* to be permitted *self-determination?* And is it not *unjust* for the U. S. *imperialists* to pit themselves against a struggle for *national independence?"*

This is a persuasive argument when Western meanings are assigned to the italicized words. But what is the revolutionary import hidden in the Communist formula for peace in Vietnam? To find out, it is necessary to translate the italicized terms.

First of all, *international tensions* can be *reduced* only by submission to Communist will. A *settlement* is *peaceful* when it furthers Communist objectives. Force used against Communist aggression constitutes *aggression. Peacefully,* of course, implies in a manner favorable to Communist aims or policy. *Negotiations* are seen as a political warfare device to obtain concessions from the non-Communist side. No *agreement* may be properly made unless it strengthens the Communists; *agreements,* however, may be broken at will by Communist, but not by non-Communist, parties to them.

A *coalition government* gives Communists legal access to key posts from which they launch legal as well as subversive and terroristic campaigns leading to eventual seizure of control of the government. *Free elections* are recognized as those that assure in advance a favorable outcome. *In due time* means, in this context, whenever a majority of the electorate can be coerced or duped into voting the Communist-supported ticket. To *reunite* implies to reunite under a Communist government. *Democratic* is a euphemism for Communist. Only those actions which promote the Cause are deemed to be *just. People* has the connotation of those friendly to Communism at a given time. *Self-determination* leads in but one direction — toward Communism. *Unjust* is, of course, the opposite of *just,* that is, detrimental to the Communist onward march. *Imperialist* is the standard epithet employed against the United States; practically, it is synonomous with "American". A struggle (or war) for *national independence* is another name for "war of national liberation", i.e., wide-scale attempt to overthrow a non-Communist government.

A translation from the Communist lingo of the proposal for peace in Vietnam might read somewhat along the following lines:

"If the United States would just do as we Communists say — stop opposing us with force in Vietnam and withdraw its troops — the dispute could be resolved to our advantage, enabling us to gain strength by participating in the government of South Vietnam. Once we had succeeded in seizing control, we would permit elections to be held — as soon as arrangements could be made to assure the desired outcome. Eventually, both North and South Vietnam would be reunited under Communist rule. Does it not promote our aims to permit those Vietnamese people supporting us at the present time to determine the political destiny of the entire country? Doesn't it hurt our Cause for the Americans to keep us from toppling the government of South Vietnam?"

Communist Aggression or Vietnamese Revolution?

In testimony give before a joint subcommittee of the Senate Foreign Relations and Armed Service Committees on May 3, 1967, Secretary of State Dean Rusk reiterated U.S. policy in Vietnam: "The purpose of the United States in the present conflict has not been to destroy North Vietnam but to end armed aggression and restore peace to South Vietnam." Mr. Rusk's statement was obviously intended to be understood in accordance with the dictionary definitions of "aggression" and "peace".

On July 30, 1967 UN Secretary General Thant addressed some 8000 Quakers at Friends World Conference in Greensboro, N.C. U Thant's idea of what is going on in Vietnam contradicts the official viewpoint of the U.S. Government as enunciated above by Secretary Rusk.

"I am convinced," the Secretary General said, "that the war cannot be brought to an end until the United

States and her allies recognize that it is being fought by the Vietnamese, not as a war of Communist aggression, but as a war of national independence."

Was U Thant expressing this thought in the idiom of world revolution? If so, he was quite right in saying that the United States must recognize that the war is not being fought against "Communist aggression" (there is no way of expressing this thought in the Communist lexicon), but as a "war of national independence", the revolutionary sense of which is a Communist-supported conflict aimed at toppling a non-Communist government.

On the other hand, U Thant may have been merely echoing the honest sentiments of many a sincere American "dove" — such as his audience which applauded his statement — believing that there is indeed a revolution taking place in Vietnam and that Communist participation in it is relatively unimportant.

Escalation — Fact or Fiction?

Sometimes descriptive labels appear on the scene that are vague and misleading; they may even be nonsense words because they have no basis in fact, referring to ideas or concepts that are impossible or non-existent. If they are analyzed, it may be found they are revolutionary terms standing for something quite different from what they seem to mean. "Escalation" and "de-escalation" are two such terms.

In the summer of 1967 a nationally prominent political figure made the following prediction during a television press interview, "If the policy of escalation in Vietnam continues, President Johnson will find it difficult to get re-elected next year." Later on in the program, responding to a question, he said, "I support a policy of de-escalation in Vietnam."

Exactly what did he mean? Neither "escalation" nor "de-escalation", its counterpart, can be found in the dictionary for they are newly-coined words. Yet everybody seems to understand their meaning. Ask anybody who has at least a nodding acquaintance with foreign affiairs what "escalation" is and the reply will more than likely be something like this, "You know it's enlarging the war in Vietnam and if we don't stop it, Red China or Russia may step in, and then we'll have World War III on our hands." How can we de-escalate the war? "As a starter, we can stop bombing North Vietnam," may come the reply.

Although it is difficult to pin down the precise connotation of "escalation", it does seem to suggest reprehensible acts committed deliberately, unjustifiably and unilaterally by the United States. How often is anything found in news reports refering to North Vietnam's escalation of the war? On the other hand, "de-escalation" appears to be a cessation of U. S. "escalation". The impression lingers that "escalation" is bad and wrong and "de-escalation", being its opposite, must therefore be good and right.

The concept "escalation" also holds forth the idea that the United States has some magical power which can control unilaterally the tempo and scope of the war in Vietnam. We can, it is implied, manipulate the course and extent of hostilities on both sides at will. If we recklessly choose to "escalate", the killing increases, also on both sides, and World War III may be just around the corner. If, however, we wisely elect to "de-escalate", the prospects for peace immediately take on a rosy glow.

It is as though the United States were operating a gigantic war-escalator in Vietnam. When we press the "up button", the fighting is intensified — and we alone are responsible for it. When we press the "down button", the military activities subside — and it is within our power to do this. It is a truly amazing deception and far from the truth of the matter, it goes without saying, because the effects of enemy action are completely disregarded.

If we are not "escalating" and "de-escalating" in Vietnam, what are we doing? What is our military policy? Since 1956 when President Eisenhower made the decision to send military advisers to South Vietnam to replace the French advisers, U.S. policy has been one of "graduated response". In a copyrighted article, "Failure of a Strategy" (*U.S. News & World Report*, May 8, 1967), General Max S. Johnson explained the policy:

"Out of a civilian 'think factory' had come a new doctrine of 'graduated response' in war. This was the antithesis of prior U. S. military principles such as the objective . . . the offensive . . . surprise . . . and economy of force.

As one general puts it, the new doctrine runs this way:

'You kick my shins and I'll kick yours.'

'Hit me in the belly and I'll swat your spleen.'

'Punch my nose and I'll poke your eye.'

'Slit my throat [and] I'll . . .'

Says the general: 'That's where the logic of the graduated response breaks down.' "

"Escalation", then, as applied to U. S. military policy in Vietnam, is really nothing but the revolutionary equivalent for the "graduated response" to the increased pressures exerted by the Viet Cong, North Vietnam, Red China, the Soviet Union and the other Communist states which have made the war an international testing grounds between the forces of Communism and the forces of Capitalism.

"DMZ" and "Truce"

It is important to remember that *all* concepts — not only social, economic, political, cultural, legal and so on — but military as well — are subject to a Marxist-Leninist interpretation in the Communist lingo. Since this fact seems to be generally unrecognized in the West, certain military incidents make "news" that otherwise wouldn't.

Take this headline, for instance, which captioned a story dealing with the heavy fighting which took place in mid-1967 in the Demilitarized Zone (DMZ) separating the two Vietnams: DEATH AND HEROISM IN THE BLOODY, MISNAMED DMZ. According to the press account, the fierce attacks of the North Vietnamese regulars had caused U. S. military officials to predict that the Demilitarized Zone might well become the Vietnam war's "bloodiest misnomer".

Let's look a little closer at that "bloodiest misnomer". In the parlance of war, a demilitarized zone is an area free from troops, equipment and fighting — a sort of sacrosanct no man's land between the two sides. Furthermore, both sides have agreed to have such a zone, as they did in Vietnam.

"Both sides have agreed . . ." The establishment of the DMZ was the result of agreement between Communists and non-Communists. As previously indicated, "agreement" in the language of revolution means, not a mutual meeting of minds, but a means to gain strength. In keeping with this sense of the term, it is perfectly proper for North Vietnamese troops to enter, fortify and conduct military operations in the DMZ. On the other hand, if similar activities are engaged in by enemy forces, they may be rightfully charged with "escalation" and a violation of the DMZ.

The DMZ a "bloody misnomer"? Perhaps so, but only from the Western point of view.

Or take American reaction to the Lunar New Year's truce in Vietnam early in 1967. Instead of ceasing hostilities, the Communists used the four-day period to re-supply their troops and improve their positions in South Vietnam with impunity, and they made scores of hit-and-run attacks. In other words, they continued carrying on such phases of the war as they thought they could get away with.

The dispatch datelined Saigon summed up Western disillusionment by stating, ". . . there were so many aggressive actions taken by the Communists during the truce period, according to an American spokesman, that the truce was something of a hoax."

A hoax? Very definitely so, but here again there was no meeting of minds when the "truce" was "agreed on". The non-Communist side committed itself to stop hostilities for four days. That's what "truce" means in our book. The Communist side interpreted the "agreement" as presenting an opportunity to gain strength. And so it could be said that both sides abided by their respective interpretations — one Communist and the other, Western — of "truce".

As Stalin once pointed out, "Good words are a mask for bad deeds." "Truce" is a good word and the Communist violations are the bad deeds.

CHAPTER XIII

THE COMMUNIST VERSION
OF INTERNATIONAL LAW[1]

Since the time of the great Dutch legal scholar, Hugo Grotius (1583-1645), the civilized world has tended to define international law as "the body of rules which civilized nations recognize as binding them in their conduct towards one another." Grotius held that international law was based on natural law, which he viewed as:

". . . the dictate of right reason which points out that a given act, because of its opposition to or conformity with man's rational nature, is either morally wrong or morally necessary, and accordingly forbidden or commanded by God, author of nature."[2]

In recent years, however, the suspicion has arisen, and continued to grow, that all civilized nations do not accept the principles of Grotius.

[1] Much of the material for this chapter has been taken from the author's article, "How Red Diplomacy Exploits International Law," published in the July/August 1967 issue of *Rally* magazine.

[2] *International Law*, Charles G. Fenwick, D. Appleton-Century, N.Y., 1934.

Double Standard

Addressing the UN General Assembly in 1961, British Foreign Secretary Lord Home posed this rhetorical question:

"Is there not growing up almost imperceptibly a code of behaviour where there is one rule for the Communist countries and another for the democracies?"

In a syndicated column dated April 15, 1966, Lyle Wilson of the United Press International, illustrated what he termed the "double standard" in the United Nations in these words:

". . . the United Nations is not impressed by the Chinese-North Vietnamese Communist aggression against South Vietnam. Article I, Chapter I of the U.N. covenant states that the U.N.'s pledge and purpose is to suppress aggression. But somehow that seems to apply only rarely to those situations deemed urgent by the United States."[3]

Speaking before a joint session of the U. S. Congress in September 1966, Ferdinand E. Marcos, president of the Republic of the Philippines, made the following observation:

". . . we witness . . . the disintegration of international law itself because of the inability of nations and powers in the international community to live by the postulates of the rule of law. The system of Grotius and the efforts of the internationalists to enlist reason and an ordered postulate of justice in the settlement of disputes have found no concrete reality."

What is happening to international law? Is it disintegrating as President Marcos suggests? Or did Lord

[3] Used with the permission of the late Mr. Wilson.

Home correctly diagnose the problem — there is indeed "a code of behaviour where there is one rule for the Communist countries and another for the democracies?" It is submitted that there does exist another version of international law, based on the tenets and precepts of Marxism-Leninism, and that it is challenging the absolute principles of Grotius. This would account for the "double standard" which is so much in evidence on the international scene today.

Stalin on International Law

Those who follow the teachings of Marx and Lenin — the Marxist-Leninists — have arrived at a version of international law which, as might be suspected, is directly related to the promotion of the "class struggle." Two decades ago, Joseph Stalin, then Premier of the Soviet Union, proffered the following thoughts on the subject:

"International law, by virtue of its *progressive* standards and *democratic* institutions, is one of the means of securing *international peace* and *international lawfulness*. . . . International law is now the arena for the struggle of two contradictory tendencies — the *progressive-democratic* and *reactionary-imperialistic.*"

Stalin's comments are significant and bear closer scrutiny because they indicate an intention to use international law as an ideological weapon. To understand them, however, the italicized revolutionary terms must be translated into Western thought. To assist in translation, a vocabulary of the Communist terms is given below. As a note of caution, it should be remembered that thoughts expressed in the Communist lingo are frequently quite repetitious.

Term	*Communist meaning*
progressive	favoring progress in Communist political and social methods; not reactionary; frequently, Communist.
democratic	pertaining to or characterized by the principle of political and social equality and hence, favorable for Communist subversion; frequently, Communist.
international	pertaining to the relations between nations under Communist guidance and terms.
peace	peace according to Communist standards.
lawfulness	lawfulness according to Communist standards.
reactionary	not favoring progress in Communist political and social methods; not progressive; frequently, non-Communist or any of its many synonyms.
imperialist	non-Communist, anti-Communist, Capitalist, or American — all with the connotation of powerfulness.

Using the meanings given above, a translation of Stalin's thoughts might be the following:

"International law, by virtue of its standards and institutions favorable to carrying out the class struggle is one of the means of securing our kind of peace and lawfulness among nations on Communist terms. . . . International law is now the arena for the struggle of two contradictory tendencies — Communist and Capitalist."

Communist China's View of International Law

The Marxist-Leninists in control of China's mainland also take the position that international law is an instrument to advance the class struggle. One of Red China's ideologists, Meng Yung-ch'ien, writing in the *People's Daily* for September 18, 1957, summed up Peiping's view with great clarity:

"The imperialist (non-Communist) nations have their own international law and the socialist (Commu-

nist) countries have their own international law. . . .
The problem is how to interpret international law;
either you can interpret it according to the bourgeois
(non-Communist) point of view or the proletarian
(Communist) point of view."

(Translations from the Communist lingo are given in
parentheses.)

In a monograph, *Red China and the United Nations,*
published by the Committee of One Million Against the
Admission of Communist China to the United Nations,
Senator Peter H. Dominick noted that the Communist
Chinese version of international law has apparently not
been codified, although this fact does not prevent its
application.

"Peiping has developed a concept of 'modern international law' which has not been openly defined," the
Colorado Senator observed, "but references to it in
Red China's publications indicate that it can be used
at any time to rationalize the world promotion of Communism."

As an example of what he meant, Senator Dominick
cited a quotation from the same issue of the *People's
Daily* mentioned above:

"We have given active support to the national independence movement of peoples (Communist attempts to
overthrow non-Communist governments) in Asia, Africa and Latin America, thus dealing a severe blow to the
reactionary (non-Communist) theory and practice of
bourgeois (non-Communist) international law in defense of modern (Communist) international law as
generally recognized (by the Communists)."

(Translations from the Communist lingo are given in
parentheses.)

In Communist eyes, then, traditional international

law is being tested by "modern" or Communist international law. In the case cited above, the Red Chinese boasted of violating with impunity the accepted norms of international law by openly interfering in the internal affairs of other sovereign states. This action, they maintained, severely weakened the non-Communist theory and practice of international law and strengthened their own version.

Communist Definition of International Law

In interpreting international law, non-Communists may tend to assume unconsciously that all nations use more or less the same moral and ethical standard in arriving at judgments. They appear to hold that all civilized men, regardless of nationality or political belief, agree as a matter of course with Grotius that "right reason" plays a fundamental part in determining rightness, goodness and truth, as applied to the relationship between nations. Such a viewpoint, however, fails to take into account that there are two interpretations of this concept. There is the usual idea that the effects of the application of "right reason" in international relations are non-discriminatory with respect to nationality, ideology and where a given event takes place. There is also the "right reason" of Marxism-Leninism which holds that reason is right only when the Communist cause is benefited.

According to international law and custom, it is obviously as wrong for an American mob to violate the diplomatic sanctity of the Guinean Ambassador's residence in Washington, D. C., as it is for a Guinean mob to enter forcibly the residence of the American Ambassador in Conakry. By the same token, it is just as morally reprehensible for the Soviet Union to re-route the flight of a commercial aircraft so as to discharge an alleged American spy in Prague as it would be for, say, a Canadian airline to make an unscheduled stop in Washington for the sole purpose of turning an alleged Soviet spy over to the FBI.

But not necessarily so in the other ethical system. From the Marxist-Leninist point of view, what's sauce for the goose is not always sauce for the gander. Before proper determination can be made, not only the ideology of both goose and gander must be known, but also the identity of the country in which the sauce is served. From the Soviet standpoint, it is apparently in perfect accord with international practice to violate the diplomatic immunity of representatives of non-Communist states, but *not* of representatives of Communist states or states friendly to Communist states. Similarly, all's fair where alleged American spies are concerned, but any state using controversial means to bring a suspected Soviet espionage agent to justice may properly be accused of a gross and illegal breach of international propriety, not to mention an act hostile to the Soviet Union. These are examples of the "double standard" to which Lyle Wilson made reference in his syndicated column alluded to at the beginning of the chapter.

Using Grotius' definition of natural law as a point of departure, one might logically conclude that the Communist version of international law could be defined as follows:

"International law serves the dictate of a right reason which points out that a given act, because of its opposition to or conformity with objectives of the class struggle, is either morally wrong or morally necessary, and accordingly forbidden or commanded by Karl Marx, author of Communist nature as interpreted by Vladimir Lenin. Custom is adhered to whenever advantageous to class struggle objectives, and the consent of non-Communist states may be obtained by force, threat, duplicity or any other means, legal or illegal, moral or immoral, which will accomplish a given objective."

In view of the foregoing, Western leaders, statesmen, negotiators and diplomats, in and out of the United Nations, might well keep in mind constantly when dealing with the Communist powers that "negotiations" and "agreements" mean, respectively, a means of gaining advantage and a means of gaining strength.

Is East-West Agreement Possible?

Non-Communists have been disappointed time after time because agreements, frequently made after long, sticky, propaganda-filled negotiations with Communist states, have not been kept. Western observers can point to scores of treaties broken by the Soviet Union since 1918. As previously noted, early in 1967 American spokesmen termed Communist compliance with the Vietnamese New Year's truce as a "hoax".

In this nuclear age, in this era of "peaceful coexistence" and "bridge-building", serious questions remain unanswered. For example, how binding is a nuclear test ban on a state which views a treaty as a means of gaining strength? What strength will the Soviets derive from the consular treaty with the United States? How will the Soviet Union become stronger by "agreeing" to use outer space "peacefully"? How will a non-proliferation treaty benefit the Cause? How long will it be effective?

If the West, and particularly the United States, fails to take into consideration the Communist version of international law and the revolutionary meanings inherent in the Communese lingo which verbalizes it, how can valid, reliable East-West agreements possibly be reached? And will not such agreements as are made continue to strengthen the Communist world?

CHAPTER XIV

SEMANTICS AND THE UN CHARTER

"The United Nations is the last hope for peace in the world."

—A frequently expressed sentiment.

One June 26, 1945, fifty-one states signed the Charter, thus establishing the United Nations. Of the 51 original UN members, only five had governments that were Communist or Communist-oriented; besides the Soviet Union and its two so-called republics, Byelorussia and the Ukraine, there were Poland, then being incorporated into the Soviet empire, and Tito's Yugoslavia. Only five out of 51 states — less than 10% of the total — even when we count the two Soviet "republics" which are independent states only in the revolutionary sense — were steeped in Marxist-Leninist values.

Two Interpretations of the UN Charter

Since there are two ways to interpret charters — the Western and the Communist — a question logically arises. How does what the five Communist states agreed to differ from what the 46 non-Communist states agreed to when all 51 signed the Charter establishing the United Nations that summer day in San Francisco 22 years ago?

112

The Preamble to the UN Charter reads as follows:

"WE THE *PEOPLES* OF THE UNITED NATIONS DE-TERMINED

to save succeeding generations from the scourge of war, which twice in our lifetime has brought untold sorrow to mankind, and

to reaffirm faith in fundamental *human rights,* in the dignity and worth of the *human person,* in the *equal rights* of men and women and of nations large and small, and

to establish conditions under which *justice* and *respect for the obligations* arising from *treaties* and other sources of *international law* can be maintained, and

to promote *social progress* and *better standards* of life in larger *freedom,*

AND FOR THESE ENDS

to practice *tolerance* and live together in *peace* with one another as *good neighbors* and

to unite our strength to maintain *international peace* and *security,* and

to ensure, by acceptance of *principles* and the institution of *methods,* that armed force shall not be used, save in the *common interest,* and

to employ *international machinery* for the promotion of the economic and *social advancement* of all *peoples,*

HAVE RESOLVED TO COMBINE OUR EFFORTS TO ACCOMPLISH THESE AIMS."

All 51 states seemingly agreed to this statement — seemingly, because the five Communist states placed a revolutionary interpretation on the words given in italics. A vocabulary of the italicized terms follows:

Vocabulary

Term	*Communist Meaning*
peoples	who favor Communist aims at any given time.
human rights	those that promote world revolution.

human person	the Soviet man.
equal rights	as determined by the Communist Party.
justice	Soviet-style justice.
respect for the obligations	but only for those that promote the Cause.
treaties	written means to gain strength.
international law	the Communist version of it.
social progress	toward the establishment and consolidation of international Communism.
better standards	as determined by the Communist Party.
freedom	to obey orders and to enjoy the Communist system.
tolerance	for Communism and Communist shortcomings.
peace	Communist-syle.
good neighbors	those that help the Cause for whatever reason.
international peace	in this context, an international climate in which Communism may flourish and expand.
principles	Marxist-Leninist principles.
methods	to be determined by the Communist Party.
security	freedom from non-Communist attack and influences.
common interest	Communist interest.
international machinery ..	Communist-directed.
social advancement	toward a world Communist society.

Using the Communist meanings given in the vocabulary, the following translation of the Preamble shows that the Communist states view the United Nations as an instrument to promote their march toward world domination:

"WE THE PEOPLES OF THE UNITED NATIONS WHO

FAVOR COMMUNIST AIMS DETERMINED
to save succeeding generations from the scourge of war, which
twice in our lifetime has brought untold sorrow to mankind,
and
to reaffirm faith in those fundamental human rights that
promote world revolution, in the dignity and worth of the
Soviet man, in the rights of men and women and of nations
large and small determined by the Communist Party to be
equal, and
to establish conditions under which Communist-style justice
and respect for those obligations deemed beneficial to the
Cause arising from agreements in writing which give us
strength and other sources of the Communist version of international law can be maintained, and
to promote progress toward the establishment and consolidation of international Communism and better standards of life
as determined by the Communist Party in the larger freedom
of being able to obey orders and enjoy the Communist system,
AND FOR THESE ENDS
to practice tolerance for Communism and Communist short-
comings and live together in a Communist-style peace as good
neighbors mutually helping each other to advance the Cause
and
to unite our strength to maintain a peaceful international
climate in which Communism may flourish and spread free
from non-Communist attacks and influences, and
to ensure the acceptance of the Marxist-Leninist principles and
the institution of methods to be determined by the Communist
Party, that armed force shall not be used, save in the Communist interest, and
to employ Communist-directed international machinery for the
promotion of all peoples temporarily in favor of Communism
toward a world Communist society,
HAVE RESOLVED TO COMBINE OUR EFFORTS TO
ACCOMPLISH THESE AIMS."

The UN's Dual Purposes

While lack of space makes it impractical in the
present brief study of the Communist lingo to translate

the entire document governing the activities of the United Nations, it is pertinent to know what member Communist states consider the purpose of the UN to be. To this end, the following translation of Chapter I, Article 1 is presented:

"The Purposes of the United Nations are:

1. To maintain an international climate conducive to the establishment and consolidation of a world Communist society, and to that end: to take effective collective measures for the prevention and removal of threats to such an international climate, and for the suppression of non-Communist acts of force, or other acts unfriendly to Communist aims, and to bring about by peaceful means, and in conformity with the principles of the Marxist-Leninist interpretation of justice and international law, adjustment or settlement of international disputes which might lead to policies or practices unfavorable to Communism.

2. To develop relations friendly to Communism among nations based on the principle of the equal rights of peoples to select a Communist or pro-Communist form of government, and to take other appropriate means to strengthen universal peace, Communist-style;

3. To achieve an international cooperation which promotes Communist aims in solving international problems of an economic, social, cultural or humanitarian nature, and in promoting and encouraging those human rights which promote Communist aims and fundamental Marxist-Leninist freedoms for all without distinction as to race, sex, language or religion; and

4. To be a center for harmonizing the action of nations in the attainment of these Communist ends."

This translation from the Communist lingo may be compared with the actual text of Chapter I, Article 1, with terms subject to revolutionary meanings being italicized, as follows:

"The Purposes of the United Nations are:

1. To maintain *international peace* and *security,* and to that end: to take effective collective measures for the prevention and removal of *threats to the peace,* and for the suppression of *acts of aggression* and other *breaches of the peace,* and to bring about by *peaceful means,* and in conformity with the principles of *justice* and *international law, adjustment* or *settlement* of international disputes or situations which might lead to a breach of the *peace;*

2. To develop *friendly relations* among nations based on respect for the principle of *equal rights* and *self-determination* of peoples, and to take other appropriate measures to *strengthen universal peace.*

3. To achieve *international cooperation* in solving international problems of an economic, social, cultural, or humanitarian character, and in promoting and encouraging respect for *human rights* and for *fundamental freedoms* for all without distinction as to race, sex, language, or religion; and

4. To be a center for harmonizing the actions of nations in the attainment of these *common* ends."

The fact that Communist states do not interpret the purposes of the United Nations in the same manner as non-Communist states may explain the existence of the so-called double standard prevailing in that organization. The struggle between what Stalin called the "two contradictory tendencies" seems to be seated in the United Nations. Under the leadership of the Soviet Union, a sustained attempt is being made, it would appear, to convince all member states, including the United States, that the Marxist-Leninist interpretation of the Charter, purposes and principles, and the rules and regulations of the United Nations, is the proper one.

In light of this fact, it is understandable why the Soviet Union would try to muster the support of the member states, and of "world opinion" in and out of the United Nations, to:

1. Condemn Israeli "aggression" against the Arab states but refuse to discuss North Vietnamese aggression against South Vietnam;

2. Censure U. S. "intervention" in the Dominican Republic (1965) but refuse to discuss Soviet intervention in Hungary (1956); and

3. Interfere in the internal affairs of the sovereign state of Rhodesia but refuse to discuss the internal affairs of any of the so-called sovereign states within the Soviet empire.

It is submitted that this situation is a reflection of an important problem which affects the people of all nations, and one that will have to be resolved some time. Dr. Charles Malik, the distinguished Lebanese statesman and former president of the UN General Assembly, succinctly summarized it during a speech made in Denver three years ago:

"The tendency has developed to dismiss the problem as though it did not exist," Dr. Malik said. "The real problem is not of war or peace, but whether the faiths and values of Marxism and Leninism can tolerate co-existence with the principles of freedom. . . . The real question is who is retreating, which values are losing ground in the world?"

Is Red China Peace-Loving?

By whose values — Western or Marxist-Leninist — should states be considered eligible for admission to the United Nations? Article 4 states:

"1. Membership in the United Nations is open to all other peace-loving states which accept the obligations contained in the present charter and, in the judgment of the Organization, are able and willing to carry out these obligations."

Is Red China a "peace-loving" state and therefore eligible for membership in the United Nations, assuming it agreed to the other conditions for membership?

No and yes.

No, if "peace-loving" means what it seems to mean.

Yes, if "peace-loving" means loving the Communist brand(s) of "peace".

What was the "judgment of the Organization" in 1966 with regard to seating the Peiping regime *and* expelling one of its charter members, the Republic of China? How many of the 121 members indicated by their vote that they believed bellicose, sabre-rattling Red China qualified as a "peace-loving" state? 46 of them did — 38%! It goes without saying that the Communist states, despite ideological and tactical differences among themselves, voted *en bloc* in favor of seating their "soul-brother", Red China, and unseating their mutual "imperialist" enemy, the Republic of China.

If China had been under Communist dictatorship in 1945 and had applied for admittance to the United Nations, the Communist bloc could have managed to get together perhaps 10% of the possible 51 votes, perhaps 15%, but hardly more. Twenty-one years later, 38% of the 121 votes were cast in support of the revolutionary version of "peace-loving".

The question posed by Charles Malik thus becomes more crucial for the West: ". . . who is retreating, which values are losing ground in the world?"

American people frequently hear the following statement made with reference to the importance of the UN, "The United Nations is the last hope for peace in the world." In view of the Marxist-Leninist conception of the term, one is tempted to ask, "The last hope for what kind of peace?"

CHAPTER XV

THE LANGUAGE OF "REVOLUTION" IN THE U. S.

"Destruction of Capitalism is the only way to
end racial discrimination in the United States."
—Stokely Carmichael

An editorial published in Denver's *Rocky Mountain News* of July 28, 1967 put into perspective the cause of the race riots which were taking place throughout the nation. "It is unnecessary to discuss whether the riots are plotted by Communists," the editorial noted. "They expertly serve the Communist cause, defying authority through use of a murderous combination of criminals and fanatics."

The class struggle to bring about world revolution is aimed at weakening and finally destroying the principle capitalist enemy, the United States. Since revolutionary activity thrives on confusion, controversy and violence, it would be almost incredible if the Communists did *not* have a hand in the riots. The question, then, should not be: "Are the Communists involved in the racial disturbances?" but "To what extent are they involved?"

Just as the speech mannerisms and use of local or regional expressions of an American from the Midwest or the South reveal the area of his origin, so do the international Marxist-Leninists betray themselves by what they say and how they say it.

How does the language of the activists, the agitators and the riot-inciters — the Stokely Carmichaels, the H. Rap Browns and the Floyd McKissicks — suggest Communist influence? Evidence of the widespread use of the Communist lingo is conclusive and it matters little whether the promoters of revolution have been indoctrinated in Marxism-Leninism or are merely repeating slogans found in the *Daily Worker*. What does matter is that these Americans, black and white, have apparently accepted the faiths and values of Marxism-Leninism and are bent on overthrowing the government of the United States. In this sense, they must consider themselves "internationalists" instead of traitors. Hence, they must feel at home in Havana, Peiping, Hanoi or Moscow, from which sanctuaries they can send back, as appropriate, glowing descriptions of the "Socialist" system in operation, fabrication about American atrocities in Vietnam, or suggestions concerning the most effective way to promote racial strife in the United States.

Americans may as well get accustomed to the idea that Communists consider that a revolution is taking shape in this country, the final objective of which is the establishment of a Peoples Democratic Republic of the United States — a Soviet America. It seems to be spearheaded by the black power movement aimed at utilizing "racial discrimination" as justification for "liberating" us from the "reactionary", "bourgeois" attributes of American civilization, i.e., the free-enterprise system, the Judeo-Christian ethic and the concept of the worth of the individual.

As in the case of all such "liberation movements", the Communist position with respect to the "revolution" in the U. S. is a defensive one. It will be recalled that

Khrushchev made it quite clear to Ambassador Harriman that any attempts to alter the *status quo,* i.e., to stop the onward Communist march, would be considered "aggression". The ex-Soviet dictator might also have added that various attempts to alter the *status quo* of a "liberation movement" could be labeled, as appropriate, "oppression", "persecution", "police brutality", "counter-revolutionary", "atrocities", "genocide", "reactionary", "Storm-trooper tactics", "criminal discrimination" or the "denial of rights" — civil, human, constitutional and even "the right of the black people to revolt when they deem it necessary or in their interests".[1] These are some of the terms employed by the Marxist-Leninists, tailored to fit the "revolution" in the U. S.

As expressed in the Communist lingo, the revolution in this country is being fought for such objectives as black power, equality, freedom, justice, to claim the various kinds of "rights" listed in the preceding paragraph, to end racial discrimination, to end criminal discrimination, to end oppression and so on.

Similarly, the developing revolution may be represented as a black revolution, a liberation movement, a national liberation movement, an independence movement, a national independence movement, a war of liberation, a war of national liberation,[2] a war of inde-

[1] This "right" was actually embodied in a resolution passed at the black power conference held in Newark, N.J. in July 1967.
[2] On August 18, 1967 an AP dispatch from New York quoted from an official announcement of the Student Nonviolent Coordinating Committee as follows, "By this visit to Southeast Asia, Mr. Carmichael joins the list of black leaders . . . who have visited this area, America's testing ground for how it will crush *wars of national liberation* around the world, *including the one developing in this country.*" (Italics supplied)

pendence, a war of national independence, a struggle expressing the will of the people, the will of the black people, the will of the oppressed minorities, the will of the oppressed black minorities, and so on, struggling for or against the good or bad things mentioned in the preceding paragraphs.

Remove references to Negroes and racial discrimination and what is left is what the Vietnamese people are said to be struggling for or against, for revolutionary terminology is standard and thus applicable to describe attempted Communist takeovers in any non-Communist country.

If riots and lawlessness in the United States increase to the point where it is generally recognized that a genuine rebellion or revolution does exist, it may be that some of the aforementioned Communist labels will unwittingly be picked up by the press and applied to describe what is taking place.

At the black power conference alluded to in Footnote 1, H. Rap Brown, national chairman of the Student Nonviolent Coordinating Committee, was interviewed by reporters. When Negroes react against conditions, "it is not a riot but a rebellion," Brown said. "Counterrevolutionary violence will be met with revolutionary violence."

Observe the similarity in phraseology between Brown's second statement and one made on the other side of the world by the leader of the Communist-oriented Malayan National Liberation League, which is seeking to "liberate" Malaya from non-Communist influence. As reported by the *New China News Agency* on January 19, 1966, he expressed himself in the universal Communist lingo as follows:

"The Malayan people (i.e., Malayan Communists)

have learned from their experience that in order to free themselves from (i.e., destroy) the rule of imperialism (i.e., democracy) revolutionary violence (i.e., riots, terrorism, etc.) is the only answer to counter-revolutionary violence (i.e., attempts of the civil authorities to restore law and order) . . ."

Brown's statement is of interest for two other reasons:

(1) He implied that lawlessness on the part of Negroes is in self-defense. The looting, arson, sniping and all the rest are a "reaction" to "provocation" on the part of "Whitey". Brown's "status quo", — like Khrushchev's, like the Arabs' in the Middle East, like Ivan's after he snatched Sammy's dollar — followed illegal acts in "self-defense". This idea of offensive "self-defense" was made clear by Stokely Carmichael, who boasted from the safety of Havana:

"In Newark we are applying the tactics of guerilla warfare. We are preparing groups of urban guerillas for our *defense of the cities.*" (Italics supplied.)

Or, as stated later by Brown in a mob-inciting speech in Detroit, "We're going to have to defend ourselves. The white man is not going to defend us."

(2) Brown does not consider rioters as lawbreakers but as "rebels" or "revolutionaries" who are obviously beyond the law. (This of course is an extension of the "civil disobedience" concept so prevalent several years ago when there was sympathetic support from many sectors of the white community for the breaking of laws considered "unjust", i.e., against the interests of the civil-rights movement.) Hence, when rioters are caught, they see themselves not as criminals but as "political prisoners". In this connection, note the revolutionary language of Floyd McKissick, national director of the Congress of Racial Equality. Following the

wave of riots in late July, McKissick said, "Release all political prisoners. Now! By that we mean those seized during the recent rebellions."

Political prisoners? Rebellions? For McKissick, too, they were not riots but "rebellions". The looters, the Molotov cocktail throwers, the snipers, those who stoned firemen trying to extinguish fires set by arson — those arrested for committing criminal acts against society — are termed "political prisoners" whom the head of CORE would have released! And this wasn't all, either. McKissick predicted that the summer's racial explosions might well go down in history as the beginning of the "black revolution".

There must always be some justification for Communist agitation, some spark of truth which hopefully can be fanned to start the fires of revolution. The less-justified the "oppression", the better chance there is for success. The Marxist-Leninist formula for killing the fly on baby's head is to hit it with a hammer. Thus Stokely Carmichael shows where he stands by saying, "Destruction of Capitalism is the only way to end racial discrimination in the United States." The only way, that is, from the Marxist-Leninist point of view. When Communists have a favorable climate in which to operate, such as the current one of "peaceful co-existence", or are otherwise emboldened or even indiscreet, they may disregard their lingo and express their revolutionary thoughts in Western fashion that has only one unmistakable meaning. Another instance of this was Khrushchev's open boast in 1959, "We will bury you," which Communist apologists have been trying to explain away ever since in one way or another. But Khrushchev said it in a moment of indiscretion and he meant it, just as Carmichael means it, too.

In Communist phraseology, it is "the hope of the proletariat" everywhere that "racial discrimination" may turn out to be the American Achilles' heel. The black power movement's exploitation of it could logically lead, from the Communist standpoint, to a black revolution which will finally lay low the U. S. Government.

The means? Guerilla warfare tactics. War in the streets. War in the suburbs. As Carmichael said, "We are preparing urban guerillas for the defense of our cities." On August 26, 1967 Rap Brown told a cheering crowd of more than 3,000 Negroes that Detroit rioters "did a good job" and that Detroit's riot would "look like a picnic" when Negroes unite.

When Negroes unite. Doesn't this sound like the old revolutionary slogan, "Workers of the World, Unite!"?

LeRoi Jones, Negro poet and playwright, told a student audience at Colorado State College last Spring:

"There is a new consciousness abroad among American Negroes today. The Negroes are rejecting the white society's ideals. Those gray flabby buildings; that is not our way. We mean a reordering of the planet."

Where do you suppose he got *that* idea?

There will be assistance from the misguided idealists, as well as the out-and-out subversive elements in the white community. Who will they be? In early August 1967 Floyd McKissick and 15 other Negro civil rights leaders sent a letter to several thousand members of Negro organizations urging them to attend the forthcoming National Conference for New Politics, August 31-September 4 in Chicago. (In passing, it should be noted that in the Communist lingo the adjective "new" as applied to a political organization means "Communist-oriented", e.g., the New Left.)[3]

"There are whites who are still committed to the struggle for freedom and justice," the letter stated. "The necessity for cooperation between black militants and white progerssives has not passed, nor can it be overemphasized at the new politics convention."

Thus, following the Marxist-Leninist principle of curing by destroying, McKissick called for "extra-parliamentary" (illegal) rather than "parliamentary means" (legal) to resolve the problem of racial discrimination. One cannot help but wonder what kind of "freedom" and "justice" the black militants are struggling for. Is it the kind that will exist in the "world of peace" Premier Kosygin desires for his grandchildren? Doesn't McKissick seem to be pursuing Marxist-Leninist objectives?

What is the revolutionary meaning of "black militants"? Obviously, they are those Negroes who believe that "Destruction of Capitalism is the only way to end racial discrimination in the United States."

"Progressives"

And the "white progressives"? In the Communist lingo "progressives" are people who deliberately or unwittingly follow the Communist Line.

The Russian Marxist-Leninist, George Dimitrov, speaking at the Lenin School of Political Warfare, once said,

"As Soviet power grows, there will be greater aversion to Communist parties everywhere. So we must

[3] The press reported that several known American Communists participated in the preparation for the conference.

practice the techniques of withdrawal. Never appear in the foreground; let our friends do the work. We must always remember that one sympathizer is generally worth more than a dozen militant Communists. A university professor, who without being a party member lends himself to the interests of the Soviet Union, a writer of reputation or a retired general are worth more than 500 poor devils who don't know any better than to get themselves beaten up by the police. Every man has his value, his merit."

These, then, are the "progressives".

Is the Communist cause in America helped or hindered by the statements of the American citizens who chose to exercise their right of free speech in the following manner:

"It's a shame to be an American in the year 1965."

— Staughton Lind
Professor of history, Yale University

"We want the Viet Cong to defeat the United States for international reasons. If the U. S. is defeated in Southeast Asia, this will help break American power elsewhere in the world."

— Stephen Smale
Professor of mathematics
University of California

"We are working to build a guerilla force in an urban environment. We are actively organizing sedition."

— Gregory Calvert
National secretary
Students for a Democratic Society

"We are getting ready for the revolution."

— Dee Jacobsen
Students for a Democratic Society

"To many people, Vietnam is now an abstraction, and this country has embarked on a systematic program of genocide."

> — Edward M. Keating
> Former editor
> *Ramparts* magazine

These Americans, and thousands like them, many of whom belong to one or more of the 818 organizations cited as Communist or Communist front in the U. S. Government Guide to Subversive Organizations, are the "white progressives" whose help Floyd McKissick and the other "black militants" solicit to help carry forward the "black revolution", or if you please, the "American revolution".

Gus Hall, chairman of the Communist Party, U.S.A., however, is so confident of victory that he doesn't think front organizations are needed, at least to gain the assistance of college students in promoting revolutionary objectives.

"We're winning," he said, "Fronts are a thing of the past. We've got the W.E.B. DeBois Clubs, the Student Nonviolent Coordinating Committee and the Students for a Democratic Society going for us, but they're not 'fronts' in the usual sense of the word. They're just part of the 'responsible left'."

It can't happen here? It *is* happening — right now — isn't the lingo employed by the revolutionary leaders proof enough?

CHAPTER XVI

UNDERSTANDING THE COMMUNIST LINGO

> "For it is a peculiar weakness of the Communist propoganda vehicle that each phrase reveals its hidden motive; such a flaw should be of inestimable value to the West."
> —*Behind the Iron Curtain* by
> Joseph S. Roucek and Kenneth V. Lottich
> (The Caxton Printers, Ltd.
> Caldwell, Idaho, 1964.)

It is emphasized that the Communist lingo was devised and perfected as a political warfare weapon for the sole purpose of promoting world revolution. As such, it is inextricably intertwined with ideas concerning the conquest and domination of all nations on earth. Without its firm ideological bases — the Marxist-Leninist beliefs and precepts — this revolutionary idiom would be an inconsistent, ineffective and unreliable communications system.

If, therefore, Communists ever renounced their basic goal, the main pillars sustaining their lingo would collapse. In this event, there would be no need for a double standard in words, ideas, values and intentions. Western truth would replace the truth of political expediency because there would then be no ulterior purpose to Communist policy. When the class struggle in all its varied manifestations had ended, the Soviet Union, Red China and the United States could become friends — in the normal sense of the word — with each other and other nations. However, the atheistic, opportunist, Marxist-Leninist ethical standard would have to give way to the one used by civilized nations. In effect, all this would amount to an admission of the superiority of the capitalist system and its values over the Socialist (Communist) system and its values.

Until Communists give up Communism, then, their lingo will prosper.

Carried to the other extreme, it is not beyond the realm of possibility that some day the absolute meanings of national languages could be replaced by the Marxist-Leninist import altogether. But this could happen only if the class struggle should end in total Communist victory, for an effective control of all national and international communications media would be essential.

George Orwell foresaw this possibility. In his sobering and ominous portrayal of British Socialism carried to the extreme, *Nineteen Eighty-four,* the Communist idiom reaches the ultimate of perfection. The traditional, democratic meanings of linguistic terms, which Orwell calls *Oldspeak,* have been completely erased from the English language in favor of *Newspeak* containing either new terms or old ones with ideological import. With these and certain structural changes made in the English language, it becomes impossible for people to express thoughts or ideas contrary to the will of the Communist Party.

It is suggested that neither a "hard policy" nor a "soft policy" is required to check, then reverse, the Communist drive toward global dictatorship. Rather, what appears to be needed more than anything else is a "realistic policy", resting on a thorough knowledge of Communism, the Marxist-Leninist mentality and the Communist lingo.

The class struggle, the existence of which seems to be largely unrecognized by the average American, is an unfamiliar kind of warfare. In any conventional war, and even more so in the unconventional "Communist War", communications are vital because they transmit the enemy's plans. Their double-valued lingo is the open code in which Communists reveal all. We can tap this code, if we will, by familiarizing ourselves with the revolutionary significance of Communist speech.

If we would understand the Communist lingo, we must first of all stop assuming, consciously or subconsciously, that Communists are just like us and therefore use language for the same purpose we do. We should instead make other assumptions not normally made in connection with languages, among which are the following:

1. The users of the Communist lingo are our enemies — by their choice, not ours — and they mean to destroy us sooner or later.

2. We must disregard completely the apparent meaning of Communist speech and devote our attention to ferreting out the hidden, ideological sense.

3. Therefore, the Communist lingo should be treated as a foreign language and as such must be translated.

4. Judgments made in the Communist lingo are all ideological in character and *without exception* are intended to promote some Communist aim.

As can be seen, the key to understanding the Communist lingo is translation. To this end, a dictionary or glossary of Marxist-Leninist terminology would seem to be almost indispensable to the average person. Translators would also do well to be familiar with the ideological assumptions which form the basis of the lingo (See Chapter V).

In translating Communist speech, attention must be centered on their special, ideological interpretation of concepts. It should be constantly borne in mind that the meaning assigned to any term is *what the Communist Party has determined it to be.* Hence, when Communists refer to such ideas as truce, peace, peaceful coexistence, aggression, liberation, self-determination, negotiations, free elections and Socialism the Western interpreter ought to make it clear to the reader that the words are not to be understood in their generally accepted sense.

Putting quotation marks around the term in question is a step in the right direction, e.g., "Radio Hanoi today proposed a four-day 'truce' to enable Vietnamese on both sides to celebrate the Lunar New Year." This device, however, is not too satisfactory unless the interpreter is prepared to go on and explain that a "truce" is a Communist-type agreement viewed as a means of gaining strength.

A much better method is to qualify the term with a brief explanatory modifier. Two such modifiers are ". . . Soviet-style" and "Communist-type . . ." Accordingly, the statement, "Premier Kosygin wants a world of peace for his grandchildren" would be amended to read: "Premier Kosygin wants a world of Communist-type peace for his grandchildren" or ". . . a world of peace, Soviet-style, for his grandchildren." Other phrases that could be used to suggest the Communist sense of concepts are:

The Marxist-Leninist brand of peaceful coexistence.

Aggression as defined in the Communist dictionary.

Liberation in its revolutionary sense.

Self-determination a la Ho Chi Minh, Brezhnev, Castro, etc.

The Communist idea of negotiations.

Free elections in the Communist (or Marxist-Leninist) manner.

Socialism as practiced in Communist states.

Using this device, the interpreter would at least be taking cognizance of the fact that considerable difference *does* exist between Communist and Western concepts. To ascertain the nature of the difference, a dictionary or glossary of Marxist-Leninist terminology should be consulted.

Likewise, in evaluating judgments passed by Communist spokesmen on various world events, it appears essential to qualify the judgments in a similar fashion. It was noted in Chapter IV that any event that takes place, no matter how insignificant, can be represented in the Communist lingo so as to have a favorable effect on the world revolutionary movement. The fact that Communists select a particular event upon which to pass judgment should indicate that they consider the event to have importance in promoting some Communist aim, goal, tactic, strategy or policy, the nature of which may not be evident to the Western observer at the time.

Consider the following Soviet judgments on four important events, two foreign and two domestic, which took place in 1967:

(1) The defeat of the Arab states by Israel was bad.

(2) The increased American bombing of North Vietnam was bad.

(3) The series of racial riots was good.

(4) The anti-Vietnam war demonstrations and their corollary, the "peace demonstrations", were good.
To bring out the significance of these judgments, they should be qualified by adding an explanatory phrase or clause such as: *for the Cause, for Communism, from the Communist viewpoint* or *because a Communist goal was set back* (or *advanced*). Now re-read each of the judgments enumerated above, clarifying them with each set of modifying words.

Here again, the manner in which the Cause was promoted, or impeded, may not always be evident to the Western interpreter.

Communist judgments are not, of course, stated so naively although in the final analysis any judgment can be reduced to an expression of approval or disapproval. Instead of coming right out saying bluntly that "The defeat of the Arab states by Israel was bad because it nullified a Soviet-backed plan to destroy the most powerful capitalist state in the Middle East," Kremlin propagandists would use a sophisticated approach.

Such a sophisticated approach might well refer to the "all-inclusiveness" of those who promote the Cause or the "aloneness" of those who oppose revolutionary aims and objectives, liberally sprinkled with Marxist-Leninist terminology. Hence the judgment on the Arab defeat might be camouflaged as: "All honest men know that the peace-loving Arab states (or people) were the victims of an unjustified act of Israeli aggression aided by American imperialist circles (all inclusiveness)."

On the other hand, increased U. S. bombing of military targets in North Vietnam might be condemned effectively by employing the "aloneness" theme, e.g., "Only warmongering elements in the imperialist police-state applaud the escalation of the barbaric acts of U. S. terrorism and aggression being perpetrated against the people of Vietnam, a people who are heroically defending their right to self-determination."

As regards the race riots in the United States, the "President" of Communist Cuba might be moved to declare: "All freedom-loving peoples support the oppressed Negro people in the United States in their struggle against criminal discrimination and unite in expressing revulsion toward the racist policies of their Fascist-oriented government ('all-inclusiveness' again)."

In an attempt to convince "world opinion" that Americans who demonstrate against the Vietnam War or in favor of "peace" are following the proper course, Radio Moscow, or Hanoi, might comment as follows: "Only freedom-haters and bourgeois reactionaries favor the genocidal policies of American ruling circles in Vietnam and oppose the exercise of civil liberties in the interests of peace ('Aloneness' again)."

Note the *motif* running through all four judgments: The oppressed (1. Arab, 2. Vietnamese, 3. American Negro and 4. Vietnamese) people struggling for self-determination, freedom and peace against U. S. aggression (if there is armed conflict) and oppression (if there is not).

A main function of the Communist lingo is to provide a vehicle for attacking Capitalism as exemplified by the United States and for defending "Socialism" as exemplified by the Soviet Union. One has only to translate the lingo to prove this for himself.

Communist Lingo Gets Into Press

Communist lingo was used profusely during the so-called "Peace in Vietnam" demonstration in Washington, D. C. in the fall of '67. Speeches, signs, printed matter and shouted slogans, with emotional impact, were everywhere in evidence. These in turn were carried by the press. An example is the speech by Ella Collins, sister of the late Black Muslim Malcolm X. *The Washington Post,* Oct. 21, 1967 reported that she said ". . . It's obvious that people don't want war. Who wants war? The old war mongers. Who wants peace? The civilized young people, white and black. . . ." How many Americans recognized the revolutionary significance of "people", "war", "war mongers", and "peace"?

It is hoped that the following glossary of Communist terminology will be useful for this purpose.

GLOSSARY of COMMUNIST TERMINOLOGY
Dictionary of Double Talk

Communist utterances are vocalized in an international lingo of double meanings which can be superimposed on any national language. The following definitions or explanations give the revolutionary, Marxist-Leninist sense inherent in many frequently used terms, i.e., what the terms signify to trained Communists. Whenever a Communist term is used in explaining the meaning of another Communist term, it is italicized. Ordinary Western dictionary meanings should be assigned to the other words used in the definitions.

Activists — Professional Communist agitators or *revolutionaries* trained as leaders, orators, propagandists, mob-inciters, experts in sabotage, espionage and terrorism and specialists in handling unconventional arms such as Molotov cocktails and acid bombs, who engage in activities leading to the weakening or overthrow of non-Communist governments. Trained in Communist countries, they are usually nationals of the country in which they operate. Cuba is one of the training areas for *activists* operating in the Western Hemisphere. Stokely Carmichael and H. Rap Brown of the Student Nonviolent Coordinating Committee appear to be *activists* in the *black revolution* being fomented in the United States.

Agreement — Embodiment in writing of reciprocal

promises to be kept by the Communist parties to it so long as it promotes their interests to do so; hence, a means of gaining strength.

Aggression — Any non-Communist act which alters the *status quo,* i.e., impedes Communist aggression with force. Frequently applied to acts of the United States in discharge of its international rights and obligations. By definition, it is impossible for a Communist state to commit *aggression.* Antonym is *liberation,* employed to describe Communist aggression.

Agricultural Reform — Ruthless collectivization of farm properties, accompanied by *liquidation* of the rightful owners who won't *cooperate.* The word "reform" lends an air of progressiveness to this terrifying, illegal act which takes place during the *building of socialism* in a country recently taken over by the Communists.

All — As an adjective, *all* implies that every one of a given class or group is favorable to Communism. For example, *all progressive people, all honest men* and *all peaceloving states* oppose U. S. *imperialism* means that these groups favor Communist aims. Portraying support for Communism as being all-inclusive is a favorite Communist propaganda device. See *people.* Antithesis of *all* is *only.*

American Gestapo — The Federal Bureau of Investigation (FBI).

Anti-Colonialism — Communism. Hence, only Communist states are the *anti-colonial* powers and only they can have *anti-colonial* policies. Ant., *colonialism,* practiced only by non-Communist states.

Anti-Democratic — Non-Communist or anti-Communist, usually American. By calling us *anti-democratic,* Communists imply we do not have a true democracy which, they suggest, can exist only under the Communist system. Ant., *democratic*.

Anti-Fascism — Communism. It is implied that only Communists are opposed to *Fascism*. Ant., *Fascism*. Adj., *anti-fascist*.

Anti-Imperialism — Communism. It is implied that only Communists are opposed to imperialism. Ant., *imperialism*. Adj., *anti-imperialist*.

Anti-Moral — Not good for Communism from the standpoint of *morality*. Ant., *moral*.

Bad — Bad for Communism. The quality of badness is always inherent in whatever hinders the *Cause*. Ant., *good*.

Ban — International *agreement* to refrain from doing something considered by both East and West to be undesirable. May be abrogated unilaterally at Communist convenience.

Bandit — One who fights against the *Party* during a power struggle in a Communist country, e.g., in Red China, 1966-7. Ant., *hero*.

Black Militants — (U. S.) Supporters of the *black revolution* who advocate and use violence and other illegal means to carry out the eventual aim of overthrowing the U. S. Government. Ant., *Uncle Toms*.

Black Power — (U. S.) Union of *black militants* and Negro extremist groups with a view to gaining their objectives through riots, terror and other illegal means.

Black Revolution — (U. S.) Attempt of *black militants,* with Communist support, to overthrow the U. S. Government. The *black revolution* is now (1967) in its initial stages.

Bourgeois — A person, or pertaining to a person, with private-property interests. Since Communists are trying to destroy the private-enterprise system, or

Capitalism, which is inevitably doomed according to Marxist theory, the term has come to mean *enemy* in a contemptuous sense. By extension, anti-Communist or non-Communist. Frequently preceded by the adjective "petty" to intensify the overtones of contempt. Ant., *Socialist*.

Bourgeois Governments — The governments of democratic states. Ant., *Socialist* governments.

Bourgeoisie — The people making up the private-enterprise society marked for destruction by the Communists; hence, the *enemy*. Ant., the *proletariat*.

Bourgeois Ideologists — Those who speak or write with knowledge against Communism. Ant., Soviet, Chinese, etc., *ideologists*.

Bourgeois International Law — Traditional, Western international law. Ant., *modern* or *proletarian* international law.

Bourgeois Landlords — Private-property owners in the free-enterprise society. By extension, U. S. businessmen, industrialists, leaders and statesmen.

Bourgeois Morality — Western morality. Ant., *proletarian morality*.

Breathing Space — Obsolete term originated by Lenin to denote a lull in the more violent stages of the *class struggle* against a stronger *enemy* during which time the Communists use less obvious means to continue the struggle. This term was expanded and superseded by *peaceful coexistence* under Khrushchev and his successors in the Kremlin.

Build Socialism — Build Communism; communize; establish a Communist dictatorship.

Capitalism — The free-enterprise society marked for destruction; the *enemy*; the non-Communist world in general and specifically the United States. According to theoretical Communism, or *Marxism,* there are five phases to human society, which *historically* follow one another:

(1) The primitive society which had no private property, class divisions or states.

(2) The slave-holding society.

(3) The feudal society with its inequality of classes.

(4) *Capitalism* in which the workers are exploited by the *bourgeoisie.* The workers will allegedly revolt spontaneously, overthrow their "oppressors" and destroy *Capitalism.* Although the destruction of *Capitalism* is held to be inevitable, Communists are obliged to hasten the process by means of the *class struggle.* Hardened Communists pay only lip service to the impractical and obviously false theories of *Marxism.* In practice, they adhere to Lenin's interpretation of *Marxism,* called *Marxism-Leninism.* See *Communism* for the difference.

(5) *Socialism,* a state-controlled society, will replace *Capitalism.* At an unspecified time, *Socialism* is destined to *wither away* into an idyllic *classless society* called *Communism.*

Capitalist — Of or pertaining to a person who lives under *Capitalism;* hence, hostile, *enemy.* Ant., *Socialist.*

Cause (The) — The *class struggle* against *Capitalism;* the cause of world domination.

Chauvinism — Non-Communist patriotism; love and devotion of non-Soviet citizens for their own country in preference to the Soviet Union. Often preceded by the adjective *bourgeois* to intensify the connotation of contempt inherent in the term. Ant., *internationalism; class consciousness; Party-mindedness.*

Class Consciousness — Awareness that *Commu-*

nism is good and *Capitalism* is bad; willingness to follow *Party* orders without question. Ant., *chauvinism, deviationism.*

Classless Society — *Marxist* theoretical term denoting the Utopian society called *Communism* which will allegedly come into being when *Socialism withers away.* See *Capitalism, Communism* and *Socialism.*

Class Struggle — (1) According to theoretical Communism, or *Marxism,* the struggle between the *proletariat* and the "exploiting" *bourgeoisie.* See *Marxism.* (2) According to practical Communism, or *Marxism-Leninism,* a ruthless, unrelenting struggle, world-wide and civilization-deep, to obliterate all traces of the free-enterprise society for the purpose of replacing it with an international Communist dictatorship. See *Marxism-Leninism.*

Class Warfare Techniques — A broad term covering the most effective methods and means of promoting world revolution. In his voluminous writings Lenin set down the guidelines or *class warfare techniques* for this purpose. These ideological precepts and action principles constitute the "Bible" of Communism and have been interpreted and applied since Lenin by all major Communist leaders, such as Stalin, Khrushchev, Mao Tse-Tung, Kosygin and Brezhnev. These techniques may be referred to by a variety of names: tactics, strategy, campaigns, policies, etc.

In the appropriate *international political climate,* accompanied by an incessant barrage of propaganda in the Communist double-talk lingo, such techniques as *peaceful coexistence, competitive coexistence, peace movements, liberation movements* and *political warfare* are launched against the non-Communist world by *peaceful means* (non-violent and non-terroristic), *non-peaceful means* (violent and terroristic), *parliamentary means* (legal) and *extra-parliamentary means* (illegal).

Since Communists are atheists and completely lacking in morality in the Western sense of the term, they are not restricted by such normal considerations as right and wrong, true and false, and fair and unfair as we are in the Free World. Hence, even a partial list of *non-peaceful* and *extra-parliamentary means* is unbelievably shocking: arson, abrogation of international agreements at will, bribery, counterfeiting, deceit, espionage, false propaganda, genocide, illegal expropriation of private property, inciting and supporting riots, demonstrations and revolutions, interference in the internal affairs of sovereign nations, lying, murder, rape, subversion, swindling, terror, theft, treason and war, declared or undeclared.

Coalition Government — The temporary alliance of the Communist party or a pro-Communist party with other political factions in a non-Communist country to form a government which lasts until the Communists can maneuver themselves into complete control. In June 1965 Senator Everett M. Dirksen stated, "[We] must [avoid] the mistake of establishing a coalition government with Communist participation for South Vietnam. Bitter experience should have taught us that such a coalition merely defers a Communist takeover."

Coexistence — A phrase of the *class struggle;* the temporary living together of Communist states and non-Communist states in a seemingly peaceful atmosphere until the former get stronger and the latter get weaker. During this period of *relaxed tensions* the Communists strive to weaken the coexisting state with a view to eventually conquering it. In the meantime, under the impression that the Communists have abandoned their long-range objective of world revolution, non-Communist states give economic and political support to the Communist state with which they are coexisting. Red China absorbed Tibet into its empire in 1951 following a period of *coexistence.* The United States has been peacefully coexisting with the Soviet Union since mid-1963. Inherent in the concept is impending doom for the coexisting non-Communist state. See *peaceful coexistence.*

Cold War — The alternating phase of the *international political climate* created and controlled by Red *political warfare* strategists, the other phase being called *peaceful coexistence.* During this blustery interval in the *class struggle,* Communists deliberately increase international tensions, name-calling, insults and threats in an effort to install fear of Soviet military might into the hearts of non-Communist leaders and people. Meanwhile, no effort is made to conceal military assistance given to *liberation movements.* In 1960, for example, when the *Cold War* was in full swing, the Soviet Union openly gave military and economic assistance to the Communist government in Cuba in an atmosphere of undisguised hatred and hostility and dared the United States to do anything about it.

Colonialism — The Communist fiction that the United States and other powerful non-Communist states exploit undeveloped countries for their raw materials and other resources. By definition, *Colonialism* cannot be practiced by Communist states. Ant., *anti-Colonialism.*

Colonial Powers — The United States and other powerful non-Communist states. Although the Soviet

Union possesses the largest colonial empire in history and is striving to expand it to include the earth, it does not consider itself a *colonial power*.

Communism — There are two kinds of Communism: (1) theoretical *Marxism* and (2) practical *Marxism-Leninism*. The hidden, revolutionary meaning of Communism is *Marxism-Leninism*. The non-Communist world apparently confuses the normal meaning of Communism (idealistic, theoretical *Marxism*) with its revolutionary meaning (ruthless, practical *Marxism-Leninism*).

(1) *Marxism:* Theoretically, Communism is the second part of the fifth and last stage of the development of society. See *Capitalism* for the five stages. See also *Socialism*. Communism is envisioned as a Utopian paradise, a *classless society* in which the common man will come into his own, after the dictatorial state controls of *Socialism* have been voluntarily lifted by the Communist Party and the state has *withered away*. All people everywhere will allegedly be free, equal, happy and industrious. Peace, prosperity and progress will reign forever in all parts of the earth. All nations will manage somehow to work and live harmoniously together and presumably the world's complicated economic and social system will operate efficiently until the end of time.

These ideas were put together by a 19th century German philosopher-economist, Karl Marx, who is considered to be the founder of Communism. As ridiculous as this rosy description of the impossible may sound, it has an almost irresistible appeal to man's finest instincts and deepest yearnings. Millions of people have been, and continue to be, propagandized into lending their support to the noble cause of improving man's lot. Their support has gone, however, to the cause of world revolution, *Marxism-Leninism*.

(2) *Marxism-Leninism:* Practically, Communism is a totalitarian dictatorship operated by the cleverest, most politically agile and best indoctrinated *Party* opportunists who understand perfectly the vast difference between theoretical and practical Communism. They fully realize that *Marxism-Leninism* is a dynamic, destructive and deceitful force which, in the guise of helping mankind, is manipulated to extend control over all nations. However, to maintain themselves in power, these cynical leaders are obliged to pretend to believe the cruel fiction that Communism is a force for the good.

This brand of Communism was largely the brainchild of a shrewd, unscrupulous Bolshevik named Nikolai Lenin (1870-1924), now the revered god-hero of the Soviet Union and all Communists. It was Lenin who engineered the overthrow of the legitimate, democratic government which had been elected following the successful revolution against Tsar Nicholas II in 1917. Under his direction, the Bolshevik minority imposed its will on the majority and thus the Union of Soviet Socialist Republics was established. This was the first Communist takeover in history and Lenin became the first Communist dictator.

Lenin had come to realize that although Marx's theories were impractical, they were nevertheless invaluable aids to seizing power because of their irresistible appeal. He was a prolific writer and set down his views on the most effective ways to seize and communize territory. Since Lenin's death in 1924, *Party* leaders have been "interpreting Lenin" and applying their findings to the problem at hand — how to overthrow non-Communist governments and keep the people in subjugation.

Communist — *Marxist; Marxist-Leninist;* of or pertaining to theoretical or practical Communism. A person who believes in Communism in theory or in practice; whether or not he is a so-called card-carrying Communist is irrelevent — it is his beliefs and actions that mark him as a Communist and make him valuable to the *Cause*.

Competitive Coexistence — A *class warfare technique* meaning "Competing with us Communists while awaiting your doom." See *coexistence.* It is an aspect of the *class struggle* taking place during a period of *peaceful coexistence,* during which the Soviet bloc tries to increase its strength while simultaneously weakening the United States. The emphasis is on achieving superiority over us in some field of human activity, or failing this, making it appear they are superior. The Soviet Union concentrates particularly on economic development; science and technology, principally in nuclear and outer-space achievements; the weaponry of war; and the political control of neutral nations. Communists hold that their task of conquering the world will be easier if the impression can be created that the *Socialist* system is better than the free-enterprise system. This is why, for instance, the Soviet Union attaches great importance to winning international athletic contests — an athletic victory is a political victory for Communism.

In their pitch to win over neutral nations, the Reds employ unrestricted economic warfare, including "dumping", preferential treatment where advantageous, and other unfair trade practices. Propagandists loudly praise Soviet *humanitarianism* in extending *ruble aid* to undeveloped countries while roundly condemning *dollar imperialism.*

Convention — An international *agreement,* usually less formal than a *treaty,* to be broken at Communist convenience.

Cooperation — Collective action for Communist benefit.

Corrective Labor — Forced or slave labor performed by *enemies of the state* in *Socialist* countries.

Corrective Labor Camps — Slave labor or concentration camps where "uncooperative" citizens are overworked, underfed, wretchedly housed and tortured. Khrushchev tried to convince the world that these concentration camps no longer existed after the death of Stalin, yet to this date no UN inspection teams have been permitted to visit the Soviet Union to find out.

Counterrevolution — Revolt against a Communist regime usually before firm control has been established. Since what the Communists are doing is considered to be a revolution, efforts to overthrow the regime are deemed to be a *counterrevolution.*

Counterrevolutionary — 1. Applied to activities which resist or counter a Communist-backed revolution in a non-Communist country. 2. In a Communist-controlled state or area, the term is applied to acts which impede the communization process. The *revolution* is not considered ended until complete communization has been taken place. The term has a wide range of applicability — from criticizing the regime to work slowdowns to armed uprisings *(counterrevolutions).*

The penalty imposed by the Communist regime for *counterrevolutionary* activities depends on the nature of the "crime"; it may be death, imprisonment, social ostracism, withdrawal of food ration card, loss of employment, etc. Persons who engage in these activities are dubbed *counterrevolutionaries* and they frequently include patriots who assisted in overthrowing the preceding regime only to find they had helped establish Communism instead of democracy. *Ant., revolutionary, revolutionaries.*

Cult of (The) Personality — Term of censure used by *Party* leaders to discredit a former high Communist official and justify his removal from office. The deposed official is accused, usually with some justification, of having made himself too popular with the common people. Ironically enough, after Khrushchev became Premier of the Soviet Union he accused his predecessor, Stalin, of having developed a *cult of the personality;* when Brezhnev and Kosygin ousted Khrushchev from power in late 1964, the same charge was leveled at him. Variations of the term are "the cult of the popular idol" and "the cult of the hero".

Cultural Revolution — Chinese Communist term describing Mao Tse-Tung's attempt in 1966-67 to purge the *Party* members of widespread *deviationism* through the terror tactics of the youthful *Red Guards* and the forced reading of the *thoughts of Mao.* At stake is the proper Marxist-Leninist tactic to follow in toppling non-Communist governments. Mao holds it should be done by armed uprisings and civil wars, while the *revisionists* believe it can best be accomplished through *neo-Khrushchevism,* i.e., by following the policy of *peaceful coexistence* advocated by Khrushchev.

Decadent — Applied only to the West. Communists hold that the free-enterprise system is destined to be replaced by *Socialism* and, hence, we must be decadent. Ant., *progressive, Socialist, democratic*.

De-escalation — Unilateral reduction of military activities against the Communist side by the non-Communist side. By definition, it is not possible for the Communist side to *de-escalate*. Ant., *escalation*.

Democratic — 1. As applied to conditions in non-Communist states and organizations, pertaining to or characterized by the principle of political and social equality for all, including Communists, and hence, favorable for subversive inroads. 2. A term usurped from the West to apply to certain aspects of the Communist system. Perhaps the best synonym is simply: Communist. Ant., *anti-democratic*, non-Communist, anti-Communist.

Democratic Centralism — Pyramidal power-structure which facilitates obedience to the dictates of the *Party* within the Communist state.

Democracy — *Socialist* state publicly admitted to be under Communist control; Communism. Ant., *Fascism*.

Deviationism — Advocacy of policy at variance with the current *Party Line*. As a result of the Sino-Soviet ideological split in 1963, both Khrushchev and Mao Tse-Tung accused each other of *deviationism*. Both claimed to be interpreting Lenin correctly as to the best way of promoting world revolution. Ant., *party-mindedness*.

Dictatorship of the Bourgeoisie — The government of a non-Communist state. Ant., *dictatorship of the proletariat*.

Dictatorship of the Proletariat — An obsolete term meaning the *Party;* the ruling clique in a Communist country. Lenin frankly admitted that under the *dictatorship of the proletariat* force and terror would have to be employed until the people learned to do and think what had been decided to be best for them. Ant., *dictatorship of the bourgeoisie*.

Disarmament — The unilateral disarmament of non-Communist states, specifically the United States, in order to bring about *peace*. Hence, the Soviet Union views the perennial Geneva Disarmament Conferences, not as an honest attempt to reach agreement whereby all nations, Communist and non-Communist, will reduce or eliminate the weapons of war, but rather as an opportunity to extract advantages and concessions from the West in the general field of disarmament.

Dishonest Men — Those who disagree with the Communist viewpoint. Ant., *honest men*.

Dissident Elements — Opposition to *Party* policies or Communist aims, always portrayed as being misguided and of little consequence. See *elements*.

Dogmatism — Adherence to *Party* policy that has been changed. Ant., *party-mindedness*.

Dollar Imperialism — U. S. economic assistance to undeveloped countries. Ant., *ruble aid*.

Elements — A small misguided or misinformed minority who oppose the *Party,* Communists or Communism. The term is always used in the plural, modified by one or more adjectives having a negative connotation, e.g., *dissident elements, warmongering elements* or *reactionary elements*. Representing opposition to Communism as being in minority is a characteristic of Communist propaganda. See *only*. Ant., *people*.

Enemy — *Capitalism;* the non-Communist states, principally the United States. Any person, group, institution, state, alliance, etc., that opposes Communism. Ant., *Socialism; peaceloving* plus noun.

Enemy of the People — In a *Socialist* state, anyone who opposes Communism or current *Party* policy. Ant., the *Soviet* (or Communist) *man*.

Equal — Exactly the same in measure, quantity, number or degree, except that Communists get more than non-Communists and high *Party* members get more than other members.

Escalation — Unilateral enlargement of military activities against the Communist side by the non-Communist side. Although such enlargement is in response to increased Communist military pressure, e.g., in Vietnam, Communist propagandists try to make it appear to be calculated and unjustified. The Communist side is incapable by definition of *escalation*. Ant., *de-escalation*.

Exploitation — The usual relationship allegedly existing between management and labor in non-Communist countries; the former *exploits* and the latter is *exploited*. The alleged practice of the *colonial powers* of taking advantage of undeveloped nations for their own selfish interests. This is a one-way term never applied to Communist activity.

Extra-Parliamentary Means — Illegal means employed by Communists to carry forward the *class struggle*. Ant., *parliamentary means*.

Fair — Advantageous to the *Cause;* Ant., *unfair*.

False — Same as our dictionary sense, except that the quality of falsity is always present when the *Cause* is being hindered. Ant., *true*.

Fascist — *Anti-Communist; imperialist; anti-democratic*. Ant., *Socialist; democratic*. Although Germany under Hitler is now propagandized by the Communists as a Fascist state, actually it was an extreme form of National Socialism.

Fascist Bosses — Non-Communist leaders, especially American. Ant., *progressive* leaders; *Socialist* statesmen.

Feudal Lords — Non-Communist leaders, especially American. Apparently intended for the people of the undeveloped and *uncommitted nations,* the term conveys the suggestion that the United States is an exploiting society. Ant., *Party* leaders; *Socialist* leaders.

Forces of Freedom —Those that support Communist aims.

Forces of Oppression — Those that oppose Communist aims.

Forces of Peace — Those that support Communist aims.

Forces of Progress — Those that support Communist aims.

Forces of Reaction — Those that oppose Communist aims.

Forces of Reason — Those that support Communist aims.

Fraternal — Communist, pro-Communist or fellow-traveling. Ant., *peacehating; enemy; reactionary*.

Freedom — Quality or state of being free to obey Party orders. The ultimate in *freedom* will have been reached when the *Soviet man* learns to enjoy following *Party* dictates. Ant., *oppression*.

Free Elections — Those that offer assurance in advance of a favorable outcome. Coercion, duplicity and a single slate of candidates, depending on the degree of Communist political control, are among the means of assuring victory for the Communist of Communist-backed ticket. Ant., *bourgeois* elections.

Freedom Fighters — *Internationalists* or *activists* who fight literally or figuratively for the *Cause.* They may attack U. S. policy at a Denver University *teach-in,* be instigators of a Detroit race riot or a mass *peace* demonstration, or they may actually fight against their own government, e.g., Viet Cong and *black militants*.

Good — Good for Communism. The quality of goodness is always inherent in whatever promotes the *Cause.* Ant., *bad.*

Gorillas — Anti-Communist military leaders fighting against a Communist takeover.

Hero — One who fights for the *Party* during a power struggle in a Communist country, e.g., in Red China in 1966-7. One who makes some significant contribution to Communism or a Communist goal. Ant., *bandit; hooligan.*

Historical — Inevitable. Communists are so confident of emerging victorious in the struggle with *Capitalism* that they consider this future event already *historical.*

Honest Men — Those who agree with the Communist viewpoint. Ant., *dishonest men.*

Hooligan — Rowdy individual who breaks laws in a Communist state. Since the term is of Western (Irish) origin, it is subtly suggested that Western influence is responsible for the undesirable behavior of the *Socialist* citizens who, of course, would otherwise know better. Ant., *hero,* the *Soviet man.*

Humanitarianism — The doctrine that man's obligations are limited to and dependent alone on the *Party* and Communist relations. Since the Communist Party purports to know what is really good for man, many crimes and inhumane acts are justified on the basis of this brand of humanitarianism, e.g., the systematic extermination of the Kulaks, the middle-class Russian peasants, which freed them from the hunger and suffering caused by Communist ruthlessness; since the Kulaks refused to *cooperate* in the *agricultural reform* program in the 1920's, the *Party* reasoned they were better off dead than alive and suffering.

Ideologists — Persons who interpret the theory and practice of the Communist ideology. If their views are favorable, they are called Soviet, Chinese, etc., *ideologists.* If their views are unfavorable, they are called *bourgeois ideologists.*

Imperialism — The policy, practice or advocacy of powerful non-Communist states, particularly the United States, to oppose Communist aggression with force. By definition, it is impossible for any Communist state to be *imperialist.* Communist acts of imperialism may be portrayed as *liberation* or *independence movements* which express the *will of the people* seeking *self-determination.* Ant., *Anti-imperialism.*

Imperialist — Non-Communist; anti-Communist; democratic; Capitalist; American, all with the connotation of military might. Ant., *Socialist; anti-imperialist.*

Imperialist Camp — The United States and its allies, opposed to the *Socialist Camp,* composed of the Soviet Union and its satellites, in the world ideological struggle.

Imperialist War — A war between non-Communist states in which Communists give support to whichever side whose victory promises more benefit to the *Cause.* See *war.*

Increased Tensions — See *international tensions.*

Independence — The state or quality of being as independent as the Communist Party permits.

Independence Movements — *Liberation movements; wars of (national) liberation* — i.e., attempted Communist takeovers of non-Communist governments.

Intellectual Dishonesty — Failure to admit that Communism is good. Ant., *intellectual honesty.*

Intellectual Honesty — Admission that Communism is good. Ant., *Intellectual dishonesty.*

Interests of the People — Interests of the *Party. Humanitarian* acts are performed in the *interests of the people.* It is assumed that the people in a *Socialist* state do not know what is really good for them, and therefore, although what the *Party* does to them may seem cruel and inhuman, it is actually for their own good.

International — Of or pertaining to such relations among nations that benefit world revolution; Communist-oriented.

International Cooperation — Cooperation among nations for Communist benefit.

Internationalism — The principle of cooperation among nations to promote world Communism; *international cooperation.*

International Law — International law which serves the dictate of a right reason which points out that a given act, because of its opposition to or conformity with objectives of the *class struggle,* is either morally wrong or morally necessary, and accordingly forbidden or commanded by Karl Marx, author of Communist nature as interpreted by Vladimir Lenin; custom is adhered to whenever advantageous to the objectives of world revolution, and the consent of non-Communist states may be obtained by force, threat, duplicity or any other means, legal or illegal, moral or immoral, which will accomplish a given objective. *Proletarian* international law. Ant., *bourgeois* international law.

Internationalist — A non-Soviet citizen who supports the Soviet Union against his own country. Ant., *chauvinist.*

International-Mindedness — Mental state of preferring the Soviet Union and international Communism to one's own country and form of government. Ant., *chauvinism.*

International (Political) Climate — The attitude or opinion of the Free World, especially the United States, toward the Soviet Union and international Communism, the Communist objective of world domination, and Communist activities and needs. Kremlin political warfare strategists recognize and manipulate to Communist advantage two major climates, the *Cold War* and *peaceful coexistence,* q.v.

International Tensions — A strained condition in East-West relations created by Western action or policy in opposition to Communist action or policy. Whenever, for example, the United States yields to Soviet demands, tensions are *reduced* or *relaxed.* Conversely, when the Soviet Union does not get its way, tensions are *increased.* The U. S. *increased international tensions* by forcing the Russians to remove their long-range missiles from Cuba in 1962, but the following year we *reduced* them by signing the limited nuclear test ban treaty.

During *peaceful coexistence,* tensions are on the whole *relaxed* because Communists have a more advantageous *political climate* in which to advance the *Cause* by *peaceful means.* The Soviet-Red Chinese ideological split has complicated the Soviet Union's control of the *political climate.* Peking refuses to follow the Kremlin's lead and stubbornly clings to the *Cold War climate* at the present time (1967).

Intervention — Interference with a Communist takeover.

Just — Just from the Communist viewpoint. Ant., *unjust*.

Justice — The quality of justice is not considered to to be present unless *Party* objectives are met. Ant., *bourgeois* justice.

Justified — Promoted some Communist aim. Ant., *unjustified*.

Just War — See *war*. Ant., *unjust war*.

Lackeys of (The Capitalist Police-State, Imperialism, Wall Street, etc.) — People, organizations or states that support anti-Communist policies, or acts of the United States. Ant., *honest men; fraternal parties; peaceloving states*.

Language — A "transmission belt" for sending instructions from the Communist Party to Communists everywhere in the world. Because of the *sectarian* or revolutionary meanings inherent in the Communist lingo, Communist messages are sent quite openly and without being detected by the West.

Laying the Foundation of Socialism — Establishment of firm political control following a Communist takeover; *liquidation* of entire social or ethnic groups with *bourgeois* tendencies in subjugated states. Millions of Russians and millions of Chinese citizens were eliminated before the *Socialist* regimes were firmly established in Russia and China, respectively. Hundreds of thousands of Cubans fled their homeland after Castro seized power in Cuba in 1959 and began *laying the foundation of Socialism*.

Liberation — Communist aggression; revolution. The process of overthrowing a non-Communist government and replacing it with a pro-Communist government. Ant., *aggression, intervention*.

Liberation Movement — *Liberation; independence*

movement. Although not all *liberation movements* may be fomented by Communists, all are supported to the extent possible under the circumstances. The degree, nature and manner of Communist support for *liberation movements* seem to be largely dependent on one factor: Can they get away with it? Since 1965, Soviet support for North Vietnam has become bolder and more overt as objections from the United States have tended to become weaker. Ant., *aggression, intervention.*

Liberators — Communist and pro-Communist participants in *liberation movements.* Depending upon the nature of their participation, these *internationalists* may be known by such names as *revolutionaries, partisans, partisans of peace, freedom fighters* and the *forces of freedom, peace, progress* and *reason.* On the other hand, the *chauvinists* who oppose the *liberators* may be represented as *gorillas, man-haters, man-hating forces,* the *forces of reaction* and anything else suggestive of disapproval, such as *aggressors, interventionists* and *oppressors.*

Liquidation — Elimination of opposition to Party policies by means of murder, genocide, exile, imprisonment, conversion through indoctrination, social degradation, removal of physical necessities and anything else that will effectively silence the opposition.

Madmen — Influential Western leaders who propose policies detrimental to the *Cause.* Ant., *sober men; honest men; peaceloving people; men of good will.*

Man-Haters — Patriots who resist Communist efforts to topple their government. Ant., *internationalists.*

Man-Hating Forces — *Man-haters.*

Marxism — Theoretical Communism. See *Communism* (1).

Marxist-Leninist — Communism in practice. See *Communism* (2).

Masses — *People;* Communists. A small number of Communists or pro-Communists in a non-Communist country, who follow the *Party* Line. Lenin pointed out that relatively few people are needed to justify the use of the term, *masses*. For example, a Communist newspaper headline, "Masses Favor Total Disarmament" or "Masses Oppose Yankee Imperialism," merely indicates that this is the current *Party Line* with respect to disarmament or to U. S. policy in Latin America.

Modern — Communist; *proletarian.* Ant., b*ourgeois.*

Moral — Good for Communism from the viewpoint of morality. Ant., *anti-moral; unmoral.*

Morality — The quality of that which conforms to the Communist conception of the ideals and principles of human conduct. Lenin said, "We say that our morality is entirely subordinated to the interest of the class struggle of the proletariat. Our morality is derived from the interests of the class struggle of the proletariat." Hence, it can be seen that the quality of *morality* can exist only when the *Cause* is being promoted. Ant., *bourgeois* morality.

Morally Unstable Person — A person, especially a prominent, influential defector to the West, e.g., Stalin's daughter, Svetlana Alliluyeva, who rejects Communism in favor of Christian morality; a *sick person;* a traitor; a renegade. Ant., a *revolutionary-* or *Party-minded* person; a *moral* person; a *Soviet man.*

Myth — Facts at variance with the *Party Line.* For example, during a *teach-in* at Denver University in 1965, an obviously *Marxist* participant labeled as a *myth* the U. S. State Department representative's explanation of the events leading up to the war in Vietnam. Ant., *reality* or *realities*.

Negotiate — To conduct *negotiations*.

Negotiation — A *political warfare technique* to win concessions and gain advantage from the West. Hence, Communists always *negotiate* for something belonging to the non-Communist world. Communist possessions are never subject to *negotiations*. In one of his moments of candor, Khrushchev explained the Communist conception of negotiation as follows: "We do not negotiate on the basis of the 'give and take' principle. We have nothing whatsoever 'to give' — we will not make any concessions because our proposals do not form the basis for a barter deal." Communists, then, have no intention of arriving at a fair and just solution to the problem at hand. When in their interests, they drag out the proceedings, confuse the issue and extract maximum propaganda value from the *negotiations,* e.g., the perennial Geneva Disarmament Conference. When speedy *agreement* promotes the *Cause,* however, they can act with great dispatch, as exemplified in the case of the limited nuclear test ban treaty *negotiations* in 1963.

Neo — A combining form used with an adjective or noun to refer to the resurgence of some activity considered to be detrimental to the Cause. Examples: neo-colonial and neo-Fascism.

Neo-Khrushchevism — Red Chinese term denoting Khrushchev's plan to topple non-Communist governments, particularly the U. S., by *peaceful coexistence* as opposed to the Red Chinese policy of using armed uprisings and civil wars.

Neutral — not opposing the *Cause.* Ant., *imperialist.*

Neutralization — The act of making a government

neutral so as to facilitate a Communist takeover; the state of being *neutralized*.

Neutralize — When a *liberation movement* reaches a stalemate, Communists may propose to *neutralize* the country, making possible the *coexistence* of Communist and non-Communist elements in a *coalition government*. If such a proposal is accepted and put into effect, Communists find themselves in a position to take over the government by using the *class warfare techniques* most suited to the situation. Hence to *neutralize* means ostensibly to make genuinely neutral but actually gives advantages to the Communists.

Neutral Nations — Non-hostile nations that have not formally committed themselves to either the *Socialist Camp* or the *Imperialist Camp* in the world ideological struggle, although many conduct themselves as if they have already embraced the ideals and values of *Marxism-Leninism*. Communists view the world as being divided into three important blocs: the *Socialist* states, the *Imperialist* states and the *neutral nations*. A major Communist effort is being made to subvert, entice and coerce the undeveloped and newly-established nations of the world into the *Socialist* sphere of influence. The undeveloped countries in Latin America, Asia and the Near East, as well as the new nations of Africa, are priority targets for revolutionary activity, subversion and propaganda. Synonyms: *unaligned nations, non-aligned nations* and *uncommitted nations*.

New — As applied to a political organization, Communist-oriented. E.g., the New Left, New Politics. Ant., *neo-*.

Non-Aligned Nations — See *neutral nations*.

Non-Peaceful Means — The use of violence such

as riots, illegal strikes and terrorism to carry forward the *class struggle*. Ant., *peaceful means*.

Nonsectarian — Of or pertaining to non-Communists, i.e., those not belonging to the sect of Communism.

Nonsectarian Language — The Communist lingo which conveys simultaneously two meanings when vocalized in any national language. At the seventh congress of the Comintern in 1935 it was decided that henceforth *sectarian* (Communist) terms likely to reveal the true nature of Communism and Communist activity would be disguised by using *nonsectarian* terms having a positive and respectable meaning. For example, slave labor camps became "corrective labor camps" and revolution became *liberation*.

Since 1935 this lingo has been perfected to a high degree. Furthermore, terms likely to reveal the true nature of the free-enterprise system and non-Communist activities are disguised by terms having a negative and disreputable meaning. For example, the United States is portrayed as a *warmongering, imperialist police-state* guilty of *aggression* abroad and *oppression* at home. Communists and their activities are represented favorably while non-Communists are represented unfavorably in the *nonsectarian language*. Trained Communists understand both the apparent *(nonsectarian)* and the hidden *(sectarian)* meanings and are thus able to receive instructions from the *Party* in a kind of open code. Non-Communists, however, tend to take utterances in this lingo at their face value.

Nuclear Holocaust — For the past half dozen years or so, a principal Soviet propaganda line has been to suggest that the United States will run the risk of a *nuclear holocaust* if force is used to stop Communist

166 Conquest With Words

aggression. This kind of "nuclear blackmail" has been effective in instilling fear in the hearts of the American people of even suggesting the use of U. S. nuclear power as a weapon in any form.

Only — As Communists use the word, *only* implies that those who oppose Communism are alone in a given class. For example, *only reactionary elements, only dishonest men* and *only warmongering states* means that these small censurable groups are alone in opposing Communism. Portraying opposition to Communism as being in a small minority is a common characteristic of Communist propaganda. See *elements*. Ant., *all*.

Oppression — Condition in which the *people* live under *Capitalism*. Ant., *freedom*.

Oppressors — Non-Communist governments, leaders and employers. It is, of course, impossible for Communists to be *oppressors*. Ant., *liberators*.

Pact — See *treaty*.

Paper Tiger — Red Chinese term of derision and contempt suggesting that our bark is worse than our bite, so to speak. The Chinese Communists appear to be getting good propaganda mileage from their "victory" over the United States in the Korean War, which "proves" we are a *paper tiger*.

Parliamentary Means — Legal means employed by Communists to advance the *class struggle*. Ant., *extra-parliamentary means*.

Participatory Democracy — Black Power-New Left revolutionary term meaning demonstrations turned to riots, cries of police brutality and criminal discrimination, guerilla warfare — in short, more Wattses, Newarks and Detroits — liberation, Communist-style.

Partisans — *Revolutionaries* in the guise of patriots. Ant., *chauvinists*.

Partisans of Peace — *Partisans*.

Party (The) — The Russian Communist Party. Since the Sino-Soviet ideological split became "irreparable" (1963), however, the Chinese Communist Party has laid claim to being the *Party*.

Party Line — Directives issued by the Party in the Communist lingo concerning the "line" or policies to be followed by Communists in all countries.

Party-Mindedness — Attribute of Communists who follow without question the zigzags and contradictions of the *Party Line*. Ant., *deviationism*.

Peace — The freedom from hostilities which will exist when the world is under Communist control. *Peace* is also considered to be Western policy favorable to Communist objectives. Ant., *aggression*.

Peaceful — Of or pertaining to *peace;* not resisting Communist aggression or subversive inroads. Ant., *warmongering; reactionary*.

Peaceful Coexistence — A grandiose Communist stratagem to obtain the unwitting assistance of the Free World in bringing about its own downfall. This seemingly hopeful term assumes a sinister meaning: "Doing what we Communists want you to do while awaiting your doom." See *peaceful* and *coexistence*.

An *international political climate,* alternating with the *Cold War,* in which Communists exploit the relatively friendly and cooperative spirit of the non-Communist world in order to change Western attitudes, to weaken our moral fiber and to erode our will to resist. It represents an attempt at brainwashing on an international scale. We are subtly invited to believe numerous things, many of which are mutually contradictory, but all of which promote the *Cause*. At the same time many Americans have come to believe there are two brands of Communism: (1) the relatively harmless political theory advocated by the Soviet Union and its satellites, which deserve our cooperation, trade and economic assistance and (2) the dangerous kind espoused by a militant Red China intent on world revolution by means of terror and force.

An American Bar Association study calls *peaceful coexistence* "a Communist blueprint for victory"[1] while a noted authority on Communist semantics states that "Essentially, the term is a deception to convey the impression that the world revolution has been called off."[2]

Peaceful Means — Non-violent and non-terroristic means employed by Communists to carry forward the *class struggle*. See *class warfare techniques*. Ant., *nonpeaceful means*.

Peacehating — Violently opposed to Communism. Ant., *Peaceloving*.

Peaceloving — Loving the Communist brands of peace. Not resisting Communist aggression. Ant., *peacehating, warmongering*.

Peace Movements — In non-Communist countries, demonstrations and the circulation of petitions in favor of the Communist brand of peace, although many signers and participants think they are expressing a desire for real peace.

People — Communists; people in general with the connotation of their being in favor of Communism or

---

[1] *Peaceful Coexistence — A Communist Blueprint for Victory,* American Bar Association, 1964.

[2] *Language as a Communist Weapon,* prepared by the Committee on Un-American Activities, U. S. House of Representatives, in consultation with Dr. Stefan T. Possony, U. S. Government Printing Office, Washington, D. C., 1959.

some Communist aim. In such phrases as the *will of the people,* in *the interests of the people* or all *freedom loving people,* the meaning becomes clear if the word *Party* or Communists is substituted for *people.* See *all* and *elements.*

People's Democracy — A *Socialist* state subservient to and dependent on the Soviet Union or Red China.

Persecution — The use of force by non-Communist civil or military authorities to prevent illegal Communist activities. *Persecution* is subject to *reprisal* by Communist authorities against the nationals of the country carrying out the act of *persecution.*

Police Brutality — A term employed to condemn the use of force by non-Communist law enforcement officers in any instance when the force is used in opposition to the *Party Line. Activists* are frequently responsible for inciting riots or turning peaceful demonstrations into riots so that police, national guardsmen or Federal troops are obliged to use force to restore law and order. Charges of *police brutality* are difficult to refute and therein lies their effectiveness as a Communist tactic. It goes without saying that any charge of *police brutality* against authorities in a *Socialist* state would be absurd since lawbreakers are considered *hooligans* at the least and *counterrevolutionaries* at the most and dealt with effectively and severely.

Police-State — A non-Communist state, especially when it cracks down on Communist activity.

Political Climate — See *international (political) climate.*

Political Prisoner — Applied to a person in a non-Communist state who has been arrested and detained by the civil authorities for having broken the law while promoting Communist objectives.

Political Warfare — All manifestations of *class warfare* are political to some extent by the nature of the ideological *class struggle* being waged against us. Those activities, however, which are concerned primarily with what is recognized as international politics and diplomacy are more properly called *political warfare*. The principal battlefields and strategy centers are the United Nations building, international conference halls, Communist diplomatic and consular establishments in the Free World, and any other places where East-West political interests confront each other. No point at issue is so insignificant that some advantage cannot be extracted from it for the sake of the Cause.

Examples of *political warfare* are as follows:

(1) In the United Nations: efforts to use the UN and its specialized bodies as a vehicle to promote Communism, including but not limited to the following activities:

(a) issuance of reports, TV programs, films and press releases depicting the Soviet Union and its satellites in a favorable light and subtly working on changing U. S. attitudes and feelings to Communist advantage;

(b) using the UN as a propaganda forum for attacks against the United States, Israel and other *aggressors;*

(c) making totally unacceptable proposals to reorganize the UN along lines more favorable to the Soviet Union;

(d) failing to cooperate in administrative matters, such as refusing to pay dues and assessments; and

(e) abusing the power of veto in the Security Council.

(2) Attempts to create disunity among members of the North Atlantic Treaty Organization (NATO), the Southeast Asia Treaty Organization (SEATO), the European Common Market and other non-Communist international bodies.

(3) Efforts to influence conferences of the *neutral nations* to take action favorable to Soviet foreign policy.

(4) Advocacy of the *negotiation* of East-West *agreements* affecting the peace and security of the world for the sole purpose of strengthening the Communist position, such as those related to disarmament, the use and control of nuclear weapons, outer space, military budgets, armed forces, military bases and non-*aggression* pacts.

(5) Abusing diplomatic rights, practices and privileges by creating and maintaining centers of propaganda and espionage in Soviet bloc embassies and consulates; expelling Western diplomats from *Socialist* countries on trumped-up charges in retaliation for the expulsion of Communist diplomat-spies on legitimate grounds; and by using diplomatic notes for propaganda purposes.

Political Warfare Techniques — Methods used to carry out the *political warfare* program, such as: consistently false propaganda emitted at every possible opportunity, *negotiation,* delaying tactics, coercion, subversion, misrepresentation of intentions, bribery, threats and other forms of political pressure.

Political Work — Compulsory Communist indoctrination.

Populace — *People, Communists.*

Popular — Of or pertaining to the Communists.

For example, a political party in a non-Communist state called the *Popular* Front may well be Communist-backed. When Communists refer to a *popular* uprising, it can be safely assumed the Communists had a hand in it.

Priest — In *Socialist* states, an agent of the security police trained in religious matters. He conducts religious services, maintains a church and attends to the spiritual needs of his congregation. He also duly reports his observations and recommendations to the state security authorities for their information and action. See *religious freedom*.

Progressive — Striving for or favoring progress in Communist political and social methods. Any act which promotes the *Cause* is considered to be *progressive*. Ant., *reactionary*.

Progressives — People who deliberately or unwittingly promote Communist objectives. Ant., *reactionaries*.

Proletarian — Of or pertaining to the *proletariat;* Communist. Ant., *bourgeois*.

Proletariat — Originally, the workers who were deemed to be exploited under *Capitalism;* the *Party*. Ant., *bourgeoisie*.

Protocol — See *treaty*.

Provocation — A defensive move against Communist provocation, attack or aggression.

Reactionaries — Those opposed to Communism or the *Party* Line; anti-Communists. Ant., *progressives*.

Reactionary — The non-Communist political and social methods of *Capitalism;* applied to any act which sets back the *Cause,* or to any person, group, organization, state, etc., displeasing to the *Party*. It is implied that Communism is inexorably destined to become the world social system and already *Capitalism* is *decadent;* therefore, any attempts to perpetuate this outmoded system represent *reactionary* steps. The term has a curious semantic twist, making us look as though we are already what the Communists would like us to be. Ant., *progressive*.

Reality — The *Party Line* particularly as regards Soviet foreign policy interpretation. Often used in the plural. Ant., *myth*.

Rebels — *Revolutionaries*.

Red Guards — Young Chinese Communists unleashed by Red leader Mao Tse-Tung to help purge the Chinese Communist hierarchy of members accused of *deviationism* and *neo-Khrushchevism*. Their two principal weapons to bring Party members to recant and accept *Party* policy are (1) terror and violence and (2) the *thoughts of Mao*. The purge is known as the *cultural revolution* which by the summer of 1967 appeared to be a bloody, wide-spread civil war.

Reduced Tensions — See *international tensions*.

Relaxed Tensions — See *international tensions*.

Religion — The *decadent, reactionary* practice of worshiping an imaginary diety. Lenin called religion the "opiate of the people", implying that people were drugged by religious beliefs and teachings so that they could be more easily exploited. If Communists can be said to have a religion, it is atheistic materialism, with Lenin replacing God; his writings, the Holy Scriptures; and *Party* leaders, the chief prophets.

Religious Freedom — The farce of religious freedom seems to be tolerated on a small scale in certain areas of *Socialist* states for two major reasons: (1) as a show-piece; the *Party* can proclaim to the world that there is religious freedom under *Socialism*, and (2) the religious feeling and convictions of the captive peoples are sometimes so deep-seated that it would be difficult or inadvisable to stamp them out at the present time.

In 1963 a group of so-called Soviet religious leaders visited the United States. They seem to have favorably impressed American churchmen, who received them warmly and tended to believe that religious freedom exists in Communist states. Upon their return to the Soviet Union, the Russian "religious leaders" undoubtedly reported their findings and recommendations to the security police.

Republic — A political area under Communist control. E.g., the Union of Soviet Socialist Republics, the People's Democratic Republic of Algeria, Cuba, Germany, Vietnam, etc.

Reprisal — As might be suspected, Communists interpret *reprisal* to their advantage. A "reprisal" is an act of force against another nation to secure redress of a grievance. Communist states, however, consider themselves "aggrieved" when their nationals are apprehended while engaged in committing illegal acts in other countries and thus justified in taking *reprisal*. For example, British police in Hong Kong arrested some Chinese Communist reporters for breaking the law (1967). In *reprisal,* Chinese Communist authorities placed the Reuters correspondent in Peiping under house arrest.

Reunite — To rejoin the Communist and non-Communist portions of a state which has been divided by Communist action (e.g., East and West Germany; North and South Korea; and North and South Vietnam) so that it becomes one political entity again — but this time under Communist rule. Whenever a Soviet leader promises to *reunite* Germany, trained Communists everywhere know he is reaffirming the Soviet intention of making all of Germany Communist.

The Communist portion of divided countries serves as a base of operations for the subversive, propaganda and military effort against the free portion. When all else fails to *reunite* the divided country, Communists may propose to *neutralize* the non-Communist portion.

Revolution — 1. *Liberation; liberation movement;* the act of overthrowing a non-Communist government. 2. The communization process; *laying the foundations of Socialism;* changing a social system from non-Communists to Communist. Thus it can be seen that a *revolution* is divided into two distinct parts: (1) seizure of territory and (2) the communization process.

As regards the seizure process, it may be fairly rapid and violent, or relatively slow and treacherous, as respectively advocated by Red China and the Soviet Union.

Once a country has fallen into Red hands, the second phase of the *revolution* begins — communization. The initial stages of this operation, which requires the *liquidation* of political opposition and the nationalization of properties, is called *laying the foundations of Socialism.* The *revolution* continues until the economy is completely controlled by the Communist Party and all *capitalist* characteristics and habits of the people who remain after the *liquidation* process have been eliminated.

Revolutionary — Of or pertaining to either of the two phases of *revolution;* a person who supports the Communist side in a *revolution* fomented to overthrow a non-Communist government.

Revolutionary Conscience — Mental state of accepting the *Marxist-Leninist* faiths and values and willingness to fight for them. In a more restricted sense, the term describes the mental state of those politically immature non-Communists who are prepared to support *liberation movements* in their own country.

Right — 1. Conformed to Communist justice; according to Communist duty as determined by the *Party*. In whatever they undertake on behalf of the *Cause,* Communists are *right* by definition. Ant., *wrong.* 2. Principally a U. S. term. Justification for carrying out the *Party Line.* Thus, Negroes have the *right* to break laws (civil disobedience), the *right* to riot, loot, commit arson, harass police, firemen, national guardsmen and Federal troops, kill and commit other illegal acts in the name of ending racial discrimination.

Right-Wing Opportunism — Advocacy of a stricter policy than current *Party* policy. Any viewpoint at variance with *Party* policy, once it has been established, is automatically condemned in depreciatory terms.

Ruble Aid — Soviet penetration into undeveloped areas and intereference in the internal affairs of non-Communist states in guise of providing economic assistance. Ant., *dollar imperialism.*

Sectarian — Of or pertaining to Communists, i.e., those belonging to the sect of Communism. Ant., *nonsectarian.*

Sectarian Language — The hidden sense contained in the Communist lingo, understood by trained Communists who receive the *Party Line* in this manner. Non-Communists, however, tend to interpret the same words at their face value, i.e., in their *nonsectarian* sense. Ant., *nonsectarian language.*

Self-Determination — The right of a people to choose a Communist or pro-Communist government.

Servility — Adoption or imitation of Western ideas, customs or culture.

Sick Person — *Morally unstable person.*

Slavishness — *Servility.*

Sober Men — Non-Communist leaders who, awed by Communist military might and the possibility of a nuclear *holocaust,* advocate conciliatory policies toward the Soviet Union or Red China, or both. Ant., *wildmen; madmen; warmongers.*

Social Development — Progress toward Communism.

Socialism — There are three versions of Socialism: (1) theoretical Marxist Socialism, (2) a Communist dictatorship or *Marxist-Leninist Socialism* and (3) the democratic Socialism of a country like Sweden.

(1) *Marxist* Socialism: In theory, the first part of the ultimate stage of human society's development. See *Capitalism.* This kind of Socialism will allegedly emerge after the *class struggle* has been won and the last vestiges of *Capitalism* have disappeared from human society. In this new world society the State will temporarily own, control and manage everything through a *dictatorship of the proletariat.* Voluntarily, mysteriously and at an unspecified time, the State will *wither away* into a Utopian *classless society* called Communism.

(2) *Marxist-Leninist Socialism:* In practice, the permanent totalitarian dictatorship of a state by the national Communist Party in power, subservient to the Russian Communist Party. Conquered non-Communist states are converted into *Socialist* states. See *revolution. Party* leaders have no intention of permitting their state to *wither away* for with it would go their power and privileged position.

(3) Democratic Socialism: Webster defines "Socialism" as a "Social organization based on collective or governmental ownership and democratic management of the essential means for the production and distribution of goods." Note the word "democratic". This is more or less the type of Socialism to be found in Sweden today and to a lesser degree in the United Kingdom.

It can be readily perceived how easy it is for Communist propagandists to use *Socialism* in the Communist sense and be understood in the dictionary sense. The usual meaning of the term automatically comes to mind when, for example, a Ben Bella-type strongman boldly proclaims to the world that he is *building Socialism* in an Algeria. Far from finding anything dangerous in this action, the United States is likely to provide economic aid and other assistance and quite unintentionally help establish a Communist regime!

Socialist — Of or pertaining to any of the three kinds of Socialism.

Socialist Camp — The Soviet Union and its satellites, opposed to the United States and its allies, called the *Imperialist Camp* in Communist propaganda, in the world ideological struggle.

Soviet Man — A citizen of the Soviet Union who has been trained so successfully that he enjoys doing and thinking whatever the *Party* tells him.

Spirit of Camp David — During Soviet Premier Khrushchev's 1959 visit to the United States, he had seemingly friendly talks with President Eisenhower at Camp David, Maryland. Later, when the U. S. failed to yield to Communist pressures, Soviet propagandists charged the U. S. with violating the *Spirit of Camp*

David, which seemed to promise trust and cooperation between the two nations.

Spirit of Hollybush — During Soviet Premier Kosygin's 1967 visit to the United States, he had seemingly friendly talks with President Johnson at Hollybush House in Glassboro, New Jersey. When and if the U. S. does not yield to Communist pressures, Soviet propagandists will undoubtedly charge that the U. S. is violating the *Spirit of Hollybush,* which seemed to promise trust and cooperation between the two nations.

Star Chamber Proceedings — Hearings conducted by the Committee on Un-American Activities. Since the Committee has been instrumental in making public a considerable amount of Communist subversive and terrorist activity, Communists try to discredit it by comparing its proceedings to those of the infamous Star Chamber of medieval England. The term is also applied to any court proceedings or Congressional hearings likely to uncover information detrimental to the Cause.

Status Quo — The Communist march toward world domination. Opposition to Communist expansion is considered as altering the *status quo* and therefore an act of aggression.

Summit Meeting — A *political warfare* tactic to gain advantages and win concessions from the West through a meeting of the President of the United States and the Premier of the Soviet Union.

Teach-Ins — As conducted in 1965 and 1966, a means of propagating the *Party Line* in an academic atmosphere. Advertised as student-faculty panel discussions, usually on some aspect of U. S. foreign policy, e.g., Vietnam, *teach-ins* were frequently organized and conducted by left-wing faculty groups, usually predominately from the Social Sciences. The approval of the college administration was facilitated by representing the *teach-in* as being organized and conducted by students to foster their intellectual development outside the classroom. *Teach-ins* have been described by their advocates as being (1) a setting for faculty-student interaction on a platform that is equal; (2) a genuine intellectual event; (3) rational discussion that enlightens; (4) an opportunity to involve young people in a productive search for wisdom; and (5) a common forum to examine the many sides of pertinent issues.

In practice, the panels were heavily loaded with professors, students and other persons critical of the United States in ratios running as high as 10 to 1. Frequently, known Communists and fellow-travelers participated. Communist and Socialist literature was often passed out at the door and Communist propaganda films were sometimes shown in conjunction with the *teach-ins*.

For the first few hours when most of the reporters, college officials, visitors and students were still present in the audience, there was some semblance of balance and fairplay at *teach-ins*, although the tenor of the discussion was clearly anti-U. S. As the evening wore on and gave way to morning, the criticism of the United States government, its policies, its agencies and its leaders increased in virulence. At the appropriate time, the pitch in favor of Communism began, at first subtly, and then as the hour got later and later and the audience got smaller and smaller, Communists and fellow travelers became bolder and bolder in an effort to obtain recruits from among the remaining tired and sleepy students.

If criticism were leveled against the conduct of the

teach-in, or any of its participants, *teach-in* advocates claimed their civil liberties, especially the right of free speech, were being infringed upon.

The issuance of a staff study by the Senate Internal Security Subcommittee on Oct. 22, 1965 sounded the death-knell for this slick Communist propaganda vehicle. Entitled "The Anti-Vietnam Agitation and the Teach-In Movement," the well-documented study exposed Communist infiltration and exploitation of the teach-in movement and showed its connection with the Communist-inspired anti-Vietnam agitation in other areas. Relatively few *teach-ins* have been held since their exposure in October 1965.

Tensions — See *international tensions.*

Thoughts of Mao — The written words of the Chinese Communist leader, Mao Tse-Tung, held to be the guide to proper conduct of the Chinese people. Among other things, reading them is represented as a cure for *deviationism* and *neo-Khrushchevism* to be performed under the threat of the terror and violence of the *Red Guards.*

Tourists — There are no tourists from *Socialist* countries in our sense of the word. Nobody is permitted to leave unless he is a well-indoctrinated, trusted and proven *Marxist-Leninist* or unless his return can be insured in some manner, such as by holding family or friends as hostages. The purpose of the Soviet tourist, for example, is to help create a favorable image of the Soviet Union abroad and to pick some information of value, legally or illegally, to be put in the customary report to be submitted on his return. All his movements are watched by the secret police, a standard precautionary measure to prevent his possible defection to the West.

Trade — Buying Soviet or Red Chinese goods at inflated prices in a hard currency and selling to Russia or Red China at prices below the world market price in a specified soft currency. This is the optimum of *trade* and can be practiced only with satellite states, which have little or no choice in the matter because of their economic dependence on the larger Communist state.

Traitor — A citizen of a non-Communist state who, once favorable to Communism, has recanted and now prefers to be loyal to his native land; a *deviationist,* especially a prominent *Party* leader, who openly disagrees with *Party* policy.

Treaty — An international *agreement* to be abrogated at will by a Communist state whenever advantageous to do so. However, it is expected that non-Communist parties to the *treaty* will rigidly adhere to its terms and conditions. Lenin said, "It is ridiculous not to know that a treaty is a means of gaining strength." Hence, all *treaties* as well as other kinds of international *agreements* — armistices, bans, conventions, declarations, cease-fires, pacts, protocols, resolutions, etc. — are considered as "a means of gaining strength".

True — True for Communist purposes; the quality of truth is considered to exist only when the *Cause* is being promoted. Ant., *false.*

Truth — Any idea, thought, utterance, etc., which advances the *Cause;* agreement with that which is represented by the Communists; corresponds to Communist *reality.*

Party policy-makers are, of course, aware of the absolute truth as we conceive of it, but they cynically disregard it in favor of employing truth as a flexible political warfare weapon. It is quite difficult for the Western mind to grasp this practice and realize that Communist "truth" may literally change from one day to the next if political expedience so demands.

Unaligned Nations — *Neutral nations.*

Uncle Toms — U. S. Negroes who advocate legal means for redress of grievances. Ant., *white progressives.*

Uncommitted Nations — *Neutral nations.*

Unfair — Disadvantageous to the *Cause.* Ant., *fair.*

Unjust — Detrimental to the *Cause.* Ant., *just.*

Unjust War — A war waged by a non-Communist state against the Soviet Union or any other Communist state. Ant., *just war.* See *war.*

Unjustified — Impeded some Communist goal. Ant., *justified.*

View the Matter (or Situation) Reasonably (or Sensibly) — Accept the Communist viewpoint.

Wall Street — *Imperialist; capitalist;* exploiting; monopolistic. Hence, "Wall Street bankers", "the vultures of Wall Street" and similar epithets are designed to create hatred of the United States.

War — The most violent of the *class warfare* techniques. Lenin regarded war as "an extension of politics by other means". Communist strategists realize it is possible to conduct a *war* more effectively if some other label is employed to describe the maneuvering of men and materiel, the death and destruction, and the seizing of territory. The preferred Communist cover-up label is *liberation movement* because of its favorable semantic impact. Thus, military objectives which formerly could be gained only by formally declaring and fighting a "war" in the dictionary sense are achieved by *liberation movement* without formal declaration of war. It is hard to rouse a country to the point of mobilizing its resources and manpower, making wartime sacrifices and developing a "Pearl Harbor attitude" over a *liberation movement* on another continent, and especially when we may be *coexisting peacefully* at the time with one or more of the Communist states participating in that *liberation movement*.

It is instructive to note that Lenin recognized at least four kinds of wars, depending on who was fighting whom and from whose viewpoint the war was described:

(1) An *imperialist war,* i.e., between non-Communist states, e.g., World War II, in which the Communists throw their support to the side whose victory promises to benefit the *Cause* the most.

(2) *A just war,* described as one which the Soviet Union wages or supports against a non-Communist state. The Vietnam war is considered to be a *just war* insofar as Communist participation in it is concerned.

(3) An *unjust war,* which a non-Communist state wages against the Soviet Union or any other Communist state, e.g., non-Communist participation in the Vietnam war is deemed *unjust.*

(4) The *justest war,* which the Soviet Union would wage against the United States. Presumably, the "unjustest war" would be the one waged by the United States against the Soviet Union.

War of (National) Liberation — *Liberation movement; war of (national) independence; independence movement;* attempted Communist takeover. Ant., *aggression, unjust war.*

Warmonger — Any non-Communist leader, group, faction, organization or state that acts to defend itself or other states of the Free World against Communist aggression. Ant., *peaceloving.*

Warmongering — Of or pertaining to a *warmonger;* defensive actions against Communist aggression. Ant., *peaceloving, peaceloving states.*

War of (National) Independence — *Independence movement; war of (national) liberation; liberation movement;* attempted Communist takeover. Ant., *aggression, unjust war.*

White Progressives — American white persons who support the policy of violence, i.e., the *black revolution,* advocated by the *black militants.*

Wildmen — *Madmen; warmongers.* Ant., *sober men.*

Will of the People — Will of the *Party* or of the Communists.

Wither Away — Disappear of its own volition. Apparently this Marxist term is used with only one subject, "the State", i.e., Socialism. Theoretically, the State will *wither away* into a *classless society,* Communism. This is supposed to take place after the entire world has become Socialist. Nobody, however, has ever satisfactorily explained how, why or when the *withering away* will occur, and apparently this is not too important. The very vagueness of the term is a master-stroke of deception in that it holds forth hope without being too specific. What it amounts to, practically, is to provide an incentive for people to support international Communism with no twinge of conscience. It also justifies the "temporary" existence of the Communist ruling class, the *dictatorship of the proletariat,* although it taxes one's credulity to expect that the *Party* elite would ever give up their controls and privileges and thereby permit anarchy to reign throughout the Communist world.

World Opinion — General attitude reflected by

non-Communist diplomatic circles and the non-Communist press. Communists try to convince *world opinion* that their representation of international events is true and that the real facts in the case are false.

World (Political) Climate — *International (political) climate.*

Wrong — Not *right;* not according to Communist moral standards; that which impedes the *Cause.* Ant., *right.*

Yankee Imperialism — "Yankee" is a term of contempt and hatred in Latin America. Radio Havana tries to convince its listeners that the United States is still imperialist because we once were. See *Imperialism.* Ant., *liberation; international cooperation.*